D0790678

(People Do
the Darndest
Things!)

"And I Thought I Was Crazy!"

by
Judy Reiser

Illustrated by
Randall Enos

Katalin Media
New York

JUN 1 0 2002

031
R375a

Copyright © 1980, 2001 by Judy Reiser

All rights reserved. No part of this publication may be reproduced or transmitted in any form or by any means, electronic or mechanical, including photocopy, recording, or any information storage or retrieval system, without permission in writing from the publisher. Printed in the United States of America. For information contact Katalin Media, 236 East 47 Street, New York, NY 10017-2146.

First Simon and Schuster edition, 1980
First Katalin Media revised edition, 2001

Published by Katalin Media
236 East 47 Street
New York, NY 10017-2146

Library of Congress Control Number: 00-93660
ISBN: 0-9707619-0-2

Designed by Judy Reiser

10 9 8 7 6 5 4 3 2 1

Quantity Purchases

Companies, professional groups, clubs and other organizations may qualify for special terms when ordering quantities of this book. Special books or book excerpts can be created to fit specific needs. For information, please contact: Katalin Media, 236 East 47 Street, New York NY 10017-2146.

For my parents,

Kate Reiser
and
Martin Reiser

Szeretettel és Hálával

Contents

ACKNOWLEDGMENTS

Heartfelt gratitude to my husband, Harvey Reidel, whose support, encouragement and advice helped make this project possible.

Sincere appreciation to my good friend, Moshe Lachter, for his consistent belief and generously given encouragement and advice.

I am also grateful to Daniel A. Biederman, Karla Eoff, Lillian Friedman, Richard Kahn, David Rieth, Melisse Shapiro, Linda Sunshine, James Todd and Robby Woodard.

And special thanks to all my wonderful contributors for sharing your delightful quirks, which I've enjoyed so much.

Thank you.

66 When I mail letters, I have to open and close the lid three times to make sure the letter went down the slot. It hasn't gotten stuck yet but I still have to check. 55

OWNER, REAL ESTATE COMPANY, MALE, 49

Introduction

So, all these years you were ashamed of yourself for kissing your socks goodnight. Nonsense. You shouldn't be ashamed at all. You shouldn't go around bragging about it either.

This book is not attempting to solve, define or make excuses for some of the more common or uncommon idiosyncrasies. Its intent is simply to help you recognize them, laugh at them and breathe a little easier. It should serve in comforting you that you're not the only one who checks the change slot in public telephones for extra coins or who touches the wall behind a *Wet Paint* sign to see if it really is.

It will allow you to accept or at least acknowledge that we are all loaded with meshugaas (a Yiddish word for strange, unexplainable, inconsistent behavior). When you see that silver-haired, pinstripe-suited, Wall Street banker type, it is quite possible that he, underneath all that normal exterior, is a total loono-wacko like you. Look, some of us wear our suits on the outside, others inside. That's life.

This sudden awareness will take a lot of your time. In fact, after reading this compilation of strange but absolutely true goings-on, you will be amazed that hardly an hour in your life goes by that you don't witness some of these quirks...either in yourself (who me?) or in others.

We know children have them. And in older folks, society chalks up odd and peculiar behavior to senility. If that's true, then senility begins at three years old. Of course having this marvelous cop-out, the old folks get away with this stuff like crazy...like crazy?

You'll finally understand your friends, enemies, bosses, husbands, wives and lovers a lot better. You may even decide to adopt some of the more ingenious ideas here.

You'll have more tolerance for your tennis partner when he insists on using the same ball he just faulted with for his second serve and the game is held up for twenty minutes while you both look for it.

Quirk compatibility is essential among couples. The next time you're at a party, instead of asking, "Are you a Leo?," find out whether he's a Folder or a Crumpler. It's a good way to avoid serious problems in a relationship.

This book is really for entertainment. Have a good time. Laugh. Chortle. And gasp at the quirks people are involved in. It will make your behavior seem all right. Or, on the other hand, it will point out to you how sick you really are and depress the hell out of you. Should that happen, don't worry. Just wave your hands wildly over your head, wash an avocado with soap and water and stick it in your ear. That always works for me.

" In my estimation, there are three different types of people: The Folders, The Crumplers, and The Rollers. The Folders are very immaculate. That's the way they are in real life. I'm a Folder, my wife's a Crumpler and my sister is a Roller. (That's when you hold onto it and roll it around your hand.)**"**

AIRLINE TICKET AGENT, MALE, 32

Pot-pourri

It isn't Mental Cruelty that's the primary cause of broken marriages. Nor is it Adultery, Abandonment, or Habitual Drunkenness. The first and foremost cause is *Toilet Paper*. And the second is *Toothpaste*. If she likes it going over the front of the roll and he likes it going over the back, or if she squeezes the tube from the middle and he squeezes from the bottom, those are grounds for divorce in my book. What did you think *Irreconcilable Differences* meant, anyway?

God help you if you're the wife of a guy with a rapidly receding hairline. I'll bet you a year's supply of Vitalis that you can't get your foot through the bathroom door because he's in there carefully arranging his three strands of hair (which are each twelve inches long and parted at the neck) trying to cover the maximum territory.

And you can't flush your habits away. They're an important, distinctive, wet 'n' wild part of you, so accept them. Don't worry about what people would think if they saw you in the tub with your rubber duck (quirk, quirk). It's also acceptable to be a Reader or a Non-Reader, a Single-Flusher or a Double-Flusher, a Caruso under the shower or the Silent Type. Under no circumstances is it acceptable, however, to leave the toilet seat up in the middle of the night or the shower on when the water is turned off. Remember that.

What you do behind closed bathroom doors is my business. Both Howard Johnson and I know about those towels you took on your last vacation. (*C'mon, admit it.*) Although I did try to be discreet and not touch on sensitive areas—I have to draw the shower curtain somewhere.

By the way, it doesn't matter how you squeeze the toothpaste, it all comes out in the end.

I am compulsively neat. My apartment is immaculate at all times. Everything is always in order. Lined up. Perfect. But I have one quirk that is totally in opposition to my personality. I must squeeze the toothpaste tube from the center. I do NOT, as would be expected, squeeze the tube from the bottom neatly toward the top. I just take my hand and squish it in the middle. And to make matters even worse—occasionally I leave the cap off.

COPYWRITER, AD AGENCY, FEMALE, 30

I shave the same parts of my face in exactly the same order every day. I discovered this just the other day. I started to shave another way and I had disfunction, I just couldn't do it.

ATTORNEY, MALE, 27

I like the toilet paper and the paper towels to hang toward the front and the maid likes it to hang toward the back. So every week she comes and hangs it toward the back and when I get home, I take it off and hang it toward the front. We have this running battle.

PRESIDENT, ADVERTISING AGENCY, MALE, 35

My friend dries his toothbrush every morning because he hates when the excess water dribbles off the brush and leaves a white film on the side of the toothbrush rack. He's meticulously clean. He recently got married and now he dries his wife's toothbrush too because she refuses to do it.

GRADUATE STUDENT, MALE, 26
HIS FRIEND IS A GRADUATE STUDENT, 26

I won't drink any water at all from the bathroom sink, only the kitchen sink. To me, in my mind, it's different water. It could never be as clean because I associate it with toilets.

HOUSEWIFE, 36

A friend of mine keeps a cigar in the bathroom. Whenever he finishes using the toilet, he'll light the cigar, take a few puffs and leave. That's the only time he ever smokes.

ACCOUNT EXECUTIVE, PRINTING, MALE, 56
HIS FRIEND IS A MANAGER, PLUMBING SUPPLY CONCERN, 56

I get up two or three times during the night and go into the bathroom and brush and floss my teeth. I'm very particular about my teeth. I've always been that way. I take constant care of them, twenty-four hours around the clock.

COSMETOLOGIST, MALE, 29

No man likes to have anyone use his razor. My wife doesn't understand that. I tried buying her the same razor I use but it didn't help. She thinks my razor is better because I use it. I tried switching. I thought that if I took the razor I bought for her and put it where I usually keep my own, she would think it was my razor and use it. It didn't work. She always finds my razor no matter where I hide it. She often drops my razor and forgets to tell me so I cut myself or she leaves it in the shower and I can't find it. It's exasperating.

FAMILY THERAPIST, MALE, 52
HIS WIFE IS A VICE PRESIDENT, PHONE EQUIPMENT COMPANY, 46

If the water is not running, I can't go. Public bathrooms drive me crazy because I can't leave the faucet on. If I'm going straight home after work or somewhere where there is a normal bathroom, I'll save it.

COPYWRITER, FEMALE, 25

After I go to the bathroom, I have to take a shower or I feel dirty all day long. I've never gone to the bathroom at work because I can't take a shower there.

EXECUTIVE, GARMENT CENTER, MALE, 41

When I was growing up, every person in my family used a towel a day, seven days a week. Of course, my mother did the laundry. It wasn't until I got to college, after I started living with other people, that I realized that some people use one towel for the entire week. I found that very strange because I was packed off to college with a huge trunk filled with towels. I was very quickly changed of that habit, however, when I started to do my own laundry.

MARKETING DIRECTOR, PUBLISHING, MALE, 30

I always use the same stall in the men's room at work. The second to the last on the right. It's the one I started with, so I just continue to use it. All of a sudden, bong, it occurred to me that I always use the same one.

GRAPHIC DESIGNER, MALE, 29

Every time I comb my hair, I comb my eyebrows. It's part of combing my hair.

HAIRDRESSER, MALE, 23

It always seemed to me that seeing one little toothbrush in a holder for six looked very sad so I fill it all up with toothbrushes. I have two bathrooms so I have ten or twelve toothbrushes—in all different colors. I always use the same one, the rest of them just sit there.

PRESIDENT, AD AGENCY, MALE, 35

I never, ever dry off in the bathroom after I shower. I put the towel around me and walk into the bedroom. For a good five or ten minutes I just sit on the bed and stare into space. Then I dry off and come back in the bathroom to hang up the towel. I just want to sit down immediately after my shower even if it means leaving a trail of water on the floor every night.

LEGAL ASSISTANT, FEMALE, 23

66 My friend Beverly needs music or serenading when she goes to the bathroom. We traveled in Mexico together and I had to stand outside the door and sing to her every time she went. The whole point is that she's embarrassed about any possible sound. 99

FINANCIAL ANALYST, FEMALE, 33
HER FRIEND TEACHES
EMOTIONALLY DISTURBED CHILDREN, 32

I never use soap. I haven't bought any in years. I use the suds from the shampoo to wash my body after I've washed my hair. It gives me nice highlights all over my body.

PARTNER, AD AGENCY, MALE, 48

I don't like to be alone in a room with a closed door, so I leave the bathroom door open wherever I am.

FEMALE, 80

I have an electric razor. Every morning after I shave, I look into the razor head to find out exactly how many whiskers are caught in the little blade, even though I don't clean it out.

PAGE, MALE, 22

Ever since I've been old enough to stand up, I've pissed outside because it feels better, it's more natural, and it keeps the sewage system from clogging up. Urine is actually an excellent fertilizer when used in the proper ratio, and if I were ecologically conscious, I'd spread it around more, but I concentrate on one area in front of my house because I'm shielded from the street there. Unfortunately, all the vegetation has burned to death. In the wintertime, I try to write my name in the snow. Frequently, I can only get the first two letters out.

NEWSPAPER COPY CHIEF, MALE, 37

I wash my face and brush my teeth before going into the shower. I feel very dirty going into the shower without having done that. In fact, once I took a shower without first brushing my teeth and washing my face and I felt so dirty that I got out of the tub, brushed my teeth, washed my face and then took another shower.

PROFESSIONAL FUND-RAISER, FEMALE, 27

Even though I live by myself and there's no one else in the apartment, I close the bathroom door and usually lock it when I take a shower or go to the bathroom. I think it's because I saw *Psycho* and if someone should come into the house without my knowing it, hopefully, they won't see me or hurt me!

TEACHER, REMEDIAL MATH, FEMALE, 29

I flush the loo before and after. I really don't know why.

STRIPTEASE ARTIST, FEMALE, 32

I assumed everyone in the world brushed their teeth with hot water. It never occurred to me to use cold water. I wash my face with warm water so it seems only natural to brush my teeth with warm water.

MARKETING DIRECTOR, PUBLISHING, MALE, 30

My sixty-five-year-old husband insists on bending over, putting his mouth under the faucet and taking a big slurp to rinse his mouth after brushing his teeth. That's the way he did it as a child and it's just become part of his habit every morning, even though I have disposable cups right there.

MERCHANDISE PLANNER, FEMALE, 48
HER HUSBAND IS A RETIRED EDUCATOR, 65

The only way I used to be able to go to the bathroom was to remove all my clothing, including underwear, jewelry and socks. It was the only way I felt comfortable, and still do really. I started working on changing it when I got to college—it would have been terribly embarrassing in the dorm if people had seen a pile of clothing lying on the floor. It's still a quirk at home. One of my brothers does it too. He's thirty-three and he's been doing it all his life.

PAGE, MALE, 22

" I squeeze the toothpaste directly into my mouth, not on the toothbrush. Then I zoom into the kitchen where I put the coffee machine on. Then I rush back into the bathroom and shave after which about fifteen minutes have elapsed and I still have the toothpaste in my mouth. At this point every morning I brush my teeth. **"**

WHOLESALER, WOMEN'S APPAREL, MALE, 35

I dated, (very briefly, for the record) a psychiatrist who only peed in sinks. He was concerned about the risk of splashing when he peed into a toilet. Although we dated many years ago, we're still friends, but I haven't asked him whether he still pees in sinks.

EXECUTIVE VICE PRESIDENT, COMMERCIAL REAL ESTATE, FEMALE, 47
THE PSYCHIATRIST IS 60

I wash soap. I like to get all the bubbles and dirt off so it looks nice and clean in the soap dish.

JR: *Do you dry it?*

No, it dries by itself.

PUBLICIST, MALE, 53

If you rub one side of my face going down, it would be smooth, but if you did it on the other side, it would be rough unless you rubbed in the opposite direction. It's because I shave one side down and the other side up. I just got used to doing it that way.

ATTORNEY, MALE, 33

I must have my second cup of coffee in the bathroom each morning before going to work. In fact, I bring the coffee, cigarettes, an ashtray and some reading material in with me and spend about fifteen minutes in there. I drink my coffee, smoke and read as I go. Everyone calls the bathroom Jack's Library.

MAILMAN, 30

I don't wash my hands after peeing. If I'm somewhere where there are people that I know and they can hear, I'll simply turn the water on and let it run for a minute so it sounds like I'm washing my hands. In a public john, I don't bother, I just walk right out because I'll never see those people again.

CABANA BOY, 21

I think it's vile to use a roll of toilet paper. I use Kleenex. It's much more civilized.

HAIR COLORIST, MALE, 28

I have hand towels to be used to dry only my face but any other part of me has to be dried with a separate bath towel.

STYLIST, FEMALE, 28

I shower from the bottom up. I start with my feet and very systematically work my way up until I get to my head and wash my hair. Otherwise I would be stuck with the confusion of where I should start and it would throw my day into a turmoil. This system is not without its problems. The big disadvantage is that the dirt from my hair drips down and contaminates the rest of me which is already clean. But when I started this habit, I wasn't aware of the philosophical implications and now I can't break the habit.

STUDENT, MALE, 20

When I take a shower, I dry myself from the bottom up. I've always known it to be strange but it's a habit I do automatically without thinking. Now, at this age, it's the kind of thing I want to hold on to because it distinguishes me.

HOUSEWIFE, 34

When I go to the john, I take my ring and watch off. I put them on the counter and when I'm finished I put them back on.

JR: *Why?*

I haven't the foggiest.

JR: *Have you lost many rings and watches?*

Never.

ATTORNEY, MALE, 35

I know a woman who never uses a bath towel to dry off with. She uses a washcloth and keeps wringing it out. It takes her about twenty minutes to get dry.

WRITER, FEMALE, 29
HER ACQUAINTANCE IS AN AMANUENSIS FOR A WEALTHY WOMAN, 48

I only weigh myself stark naked, first thing in the morning before eating anything and after, hopefully, eliminating any wastes from my body and never with wet hair. Psychologically, I feel better with the "thinnest number."

OFFICE MANAGER, FEMALE, 31

I wash my feet several times a day. I know it's excessive but I do it to eliminate any odor and for comfort because it's refreshing. It cools me off without taking all my clothes off and hopping into the shower.

PUPPET MAKER, MALE, 29

When I'm using the men's room, I can't use a middle stall—I must be next to the wall. I have a hard enough time with one person sitting next to me—being surrounded by two people drives me nuts. If an end stall is not available, I will go to a different floor rather then use a middle stall. Sometimes I have to go down several flights of stairs to avoid using the middle stall.

COMPUTER PROGRAMMER, MALE, 30

When I brush my teeth, I don't hang around the bathroom. I like to walk around the house and do different things like look at the newspaper or watch television. I don't like to stand in one spot. When I get enough lather in my mouth, I go back and rinse. I've never been able to figure it out.

PSYCHOLOGY STUDENT, FEMALE, 27

If there's anyone else in a public toilet, I won't go. I'll just wash my hands and leave so he doesn't think, "What is this weirdo coming into the bathroom for?" In fact, I started college when I was fifteen years old and when I went out there, I wasn't worried about being away from home, I was worried about what the bathrooms were like in the dorm. I was afraid they wouldn't be private enough. When I got there it was even worse than I thought. All the bowls were lined up—they didn't even have stalls—so for the first six months I went to the bathroom in the gas station across the street.

COMPTROLLER, MALE, 31

When we were in the service, my friend would put a washcloth on his face every time he went into the shower because he couldn't stand the water hitting his face.

ACCOUNT EXECUTIVE, MALE, 33
HIS FRIEND IS AN ACCOUNTANT, 33

Someone in my office uses four fresh towels every time she showers. One for her feet, one for her body, one for her face and one for her hair. Each time she uses a set of towels, she'll throw them in the wash. She won't reuse them.

ATTORNEY, MALE, 34
HIS COLLEAGUE IS A SECRETARY, 22

I use extra toothpaste on my central teeth and brush the most there because that's the part that shows.

MARKETING CONSULTANT, FEMALE, 33

Many times I walk out of a bathroom and think for a second, "Did I flush the toilet?" It's rare that I don't because I've been trained to do so, but I have to go back and check.

INVESTMENT BANKER, MALE, 46

66 My wife loves to watch television sitting on the pot. We have a television set in the bathroom and she watches all the soap operas in there."

PLUMBER, MALE, 43
HIS WIFE IS A HOUSEWIFE, 34

"I like to play my guitar sitting on the toilet. I do my best playing there."

MUSICIAN, MALE, 23

"I have a telephone in the bathroom. I don't tell the people I'm speaking to where I'm speaking to them from because many would be offended. 55

GEMOLOGIST, MALE, 27

I wear my glasses in the shower so I can see what I'm doing.
DESIGN DIRECTOR, ADVERTISING, MALE, 40

I dry my face with the side of the towel that has the label on it and my body with the other side. Or, if the towel has two different textures, I'll use the smooth side for my face and the rough side for my body. That way, I don't have to use a separate face towel and I have a lighter load to wash.
LAWYER, FEMALE, 34

Every day when I wake up and go to the bathroom to relieve my bladder, I go through the same ritual. As I'm peeing, I say out loud, "Only five days to go." There's always five days to go to something and I don't know quite what I'm referring to. It must have originated when I was in junior high school. I probably woke up one Monday morning and said, "Only five days to go," and felt very comfortable as I said it. It was reassuring to know there were only five days to go. Except I'd say it on Tuesday, Wednesday, Thursday and Friday, also. And now, I still say it in the morning. In fact, some of my friends have realized the beneficial aspects of this and some of them have tried it.
MATHEMATICIAN, MALE, 29

I hold my pocketbook on my head in a public bathroom and stand over the bowl and pee like a man. You would think I had a penis but, of course, I don't.
HOUSEWIFE, 36

After my girlfriend shaves her legs, she jumps into bed because she loves the way the sheets feel against her shaven legs.
SALESMAN, GIFT SHOP, MALE, 20
HIS GIRLFRIEND IS A STUDENT, 23

I can't go if someone else is in the bathroom—I must have complete privacy. This was a major problem at work but I came up with a brilliant solution, if I do say so myself—I simply hang an *Out of Order* sign on the outside of the bathroom door. The bathroom is in the hallway and there is a security guard stationed in the hallway. He finally caught on to my routine but fortunately he's sympathetic toward my plight and puts up with my little scheme.

ADMINISTRATIVE ASSISTANT, FEMALE, 33

Usually I shower in the morning but when I do take a shower or bath at night, I have to change the sheets on my bed. For some reason when I'm clean, the bed has to be too.

LEGAL SECRETARY, FEMALE, 31

I fold my dirty laundry and put it in the hamper in a very neat stack. You would almost think that it was my clean laundry. I do it so the clothing is less wrinkled, but when I put it in the washing machine it wrinkles anyway so it doesn't make sense.

FEMALE, 89

I have my own bathroom in the basement which no one else uses. When I wake up in the morning, I go downstairs to that bathroom in my pajamas, sit down on the bowl, and sleep for another ten or fifteen minutes. Then I get up and take care of morning functions, like brushing my teeth and shaving.

SUPERVISOR, CORPORATE PHOTO DEPARTMENT, MALE, 65

I always make sure, when I'm going somewhere, to bring a fresh roll of toilet paper with me. I use them as tissues because they last forever. I get strange looks when people see me taking out a roll of toilet paper in public.

STUDENT, MALE, 20

66 When I take a shower, I have a fear that a snake or some kind of reptile will come up through the pipes so I close down the drain. I usually have to take a medium to short shower as a result and end up with water up to my knees but I definitely manage to do away with the snakes. 99

STUDENT, MALE, 22

I keep an extra toothbrush in the bathroom so it doesn't look as though I'm living alone. If someone decides to come live with me, I have a brand-new, clean toothbrush for them.

MANAGER, PLASTICS COMPANY, MALE, 52

When I pee in a public bathroom, I stand as far away from the bowl as possible. Sometimes the people next to me get splashed because I'm usually about three feet away. I can't understand men who lean right over the urinal wearing a $300 suit.

OWNER, AUTO REPAIR BUSINESS, MALE, 34

No matter how urgently I have to go, whether it's at home or in the Portosan on the construction site, I have to go through a preparatory ritual before I sit down. First, I tear off a piece of paper four squares long and fold along the perforations into one square and set it on the counter. Then, I tear off three additional pieces of paper, each three squares in length folded into one and put those behind the first one. I use them in that order and if there's no counter, I hold them on my lap. I can't believe I admitted this. My wife doesn't even know about it.

ARCHITECT, MALE, 48

My girlfriend brushes her teeth whenever she eats. If we're in the car and she eats a piece of candy or fruit, she'll whip out her toothbrush and start brushing her teeth as we're driving along.

INSTRUCTOR, MALE, 34
HIS GIRLFRIEND IS A FILMMAKER, 28

I always flush the toilet twice because I think the bathroom will be cleaner and fresher.

SECRETARY, FEMALE, 44

It's important to shower from the top down, head to toe, otherwise the dirty rinse water from shampooing your hair will defile your clean body. Starting at the top and cleaning each body part successively on the way down ensures that everything ends up being clean and pure.

INTERNET STRATEGIST, MALE, 35

I have a different shampoo and a different body wash for every day of the week. I have an herbal essence shampoo, a highlight shampoo, an organic shampoo, a moisturizing shampoo, a vitamin E shampoo, a jojoba shampoo and a natural rosemary shampoo. And I have peppermint, raspberry, freshia, coconut, lavender, Neutrogena and stress-reducing body washes. I rotate them and use a different one each day depending on my mood.

STUDENT, FEMALE, 13

When I take a shower, I turn the tub part on and I wash my hands and feet first. Then I turn the shower on.

JR: *Why?*

Because that's the way I take a shower!

ACCOUNT EXECUTIVE, MALE, 25

After I go to the bathroom, I spit into the sink. I have no idea why I do it—it might be a cleansing thing.

COMPUTER GRAPHIC ARTIST, FEMALE, 27

My father flushes the toilet first and then urinates while the toilet is flushing so no one will be able to hear him if they happen to walk past the bathroom. If the flush is over before he is, he'll flush again.

PARALEGAL, FEMALE, 23
HER FATHER IS A LAWYER, 59

I go berserk if there's a hair in the sink or bathtub. It has to be absolutely spotless. I live with a gorilla who's covered with hair which makes it very difficult. I follow him around picking up after him.

STUDENT, FEMALE, 33

We were trained not to waste water in the navy because there's a shortage on board ship. So we showered in sections. We'd soap up one part of our body and only open the faucet to rinse and then shut the water off as we soaped up another part and so on until we were clean. By force of habit, I still do it that way. My sister and brother-in-law came to visit one time. They were waiting for me to finish my shower in the morning so they could use the bathroom and they told me afterwards that they couldn't imagine what I was doing in there because they heard the water going on and off. It seemed very strange until I explained the reason.

FIREMAN, 33

I work up a sweat shampooing my hair, so when I come out of the shower, I have to wash under my armpits again in the sink.

EXECUTIVE, MUSIC INDUSTRY, MALE, 55

As an unusual surprise one time, I filled the tub with Perrier water and my wife and I took a bath in it together. It took about a hundred bottles. I'd do it more often if it weren't so expensive. It felt like a Jacuzzi out of a bottle.

VICE PRESIDENT, SHOE COMPANY, MALE, 35

The minute I step into the bathroom in the morning, I turn the water on and don't turn it off until well after I'm finished brushing my teeth, combing my hair, shaving, etc. The sound of the water in the morning has a tranquilizing effect.

ACCOUNT EXECUTIVE, PRINTING, MALE, 56

" For many years I brushed my teeth and shaved in the bathtub. I decided it took too long so I grew a beard and have been able to give up shaving. Now all I have to do is brush my teeth, which I do in the shower. I have saved a great deal of time and added a couple of weeks to my life, I'm quite sure! **"**

LAWYER, MALE, 32

I take off my pants and hang them up when I go to the bathroom at work. They're good pants and this way I can sit down, relax and read the paper without worrying about getting them wrinkled.

EXECUTIVE, MALE, 39

My mother showers like a normal person but she washes her hair in the kitchen sink. I have no idea why—I never asked her. You see it happening but it's not really happening.

EDITOR, INTERNET ONLINE BROKERAGE, MALE, 34
HIS MOTHER IS A NURSE'S AID, 54

It's much more comfortable to be naked when going to the bathroom. I do this whenever I can, always in my own home. I'd like to be able to do it more often.

BUSINESSMAN, 34

When I'm all done with everything else in the bathroom, right before I'm ready to wash my hands, I turn off the light. It's automatic and just in the bathroom. I don't know why. When I leave, the light is already off.

SECURITY GUARD, FEMALE, 19

SCORE

Is your toilet training as advanced as that of these folks?

If you identify with less than seven of these: You're a little behind.

From seven to eighteen: It's as clear as toilet water. You either have a weak bladder, excessively clean teeth or you're doing entirely too much reading. You must be very well informed.

Over eighteen: You probably squeeze the toothpaste tube from the top down.

66 Most people I know, including myself, will spend hundreds of dollars or even thousands of dollars without giving it a second thought. But we will not buy Tropicana orange juice unless it's on special. We absolutely refuse to pay the full price. **99**

LAWYER, FEMALE, 52

Funny Money

There are a wealth of idiosyncrasies in this section because money is the root of a lot of quirks. Rich or poor, we've all got them.

If you have money to burn and you do it, you belong here. You've got what's known as an *Extravagant Quirk*. If your money is wrapped in foil and labeled "Hamburger" and you keep it in the freezer, you've got a *Cold Cash Quirk*. If you only buy it in a Downtown Discount Store at the end of the season on sale, you've got a *Practical Quirk*. If you only buy it in an Uptown Boutique at the beginning of the season at full price, you've got a *Foolish Quirk*.

If you get someone else to buy it for you, you've got a *Smart Quirk*. If you thought this book was overpriced when you bought it, or worse yet, if you borrowed it and didn't buy it, shame on you, you've got a *Don't-Know-a-Bargain-When-You-See-One Quirk*.

Then there are those of you who file the contents of your billfold with a system that's even more intricate than the most complex spreadsheet in Merrill Lynch's database. Oh, you didn't think that was a quirk? Think again. And you with the jars and cans and pots of pennies, you have a friend at Chase Manhattan. He's the only teller who'll put up with the 3,000 rolls you bring in once every two years. Actually, he looks forward to them. He saves them too. Some folks are always trying to get rid of their pennies. When the cashier rings up $3.98, they say quirkly, "Wait, I have three pennies!" It's called the *Three Penny Opera*. In this book money laundering is legal, literal and practiced by lunatics. To them, "new money" is preferable to "old money." Let's not forget you guys who carry a wad of bills with Washington's picture on the outside. You can't fool me. I know there are a lot of Jacksons and Hamiltons hidden in there. Ladies, don't laugh, some of you have quite a load in your brassiere, and that doesn't mean your physical attributes.

Anyway, read on and I hope you get your money's worth.

I'm crazy with bills. They must be in exact order, small bills first, large bills at the end, the heads facing in the same direction. The dirty bills are in front of the clean bills so I get rid of those first. More precisely, at the front of my wallet are the dirty one-dollar bills, then the clean one-dollar bills, then the dirty fives, then the clean fives, and so on.

PERSONNEL DIRECTOR, FEMALE, 35

I enter every one of my check or credit card transactions on Quicken with the intention of tracking it but I never review it or use it once it's entered. I even back it up on disks. It drives my wife crazy because I insist that she let me know what our expenses are.

His wife: He insists that the receipts be stacked according to which credit card company was used and in date order, and he will not pay a bill unless he's reconciled the entire account.

DOCTOR, MALE, 50
HIS WIFE IS A HOUSEWIFE, 51

I round off the figures in my checkbook to the next highest whole number. If, for example, I write a check for $23.60, I would enter $24.00 as the amount in my record book. If I realize I've forgotten to enter a check, I'll make up a figure which I think is higher than what I actually spent and subtract that. At the end of the year I can look forward to a lot of extra money left in my account.

ART DIRECTOR, FEMALE, 27

We recently moved and when the moving men saw all the containers of change, they laughed at me—it took two men to carry it out to the truck. I don't spend any of my change—I take it home and I collect it in mason jars, mustard cans, wine bottles and cardboard boxes. There must be at least $1,200 worth of change.

CO-OWNER, ADVERTISING AGENCY, MALE, 41

66 When my kids lose a tooth and I want to give them money from the Tooth Fairy, if I don't have a clean dollar bill, I iron an old one to make it crisp. I just have this thing about dirty money and I have to iron it if it's not clean and crisp. **99**

GRAPHIC DESIGNER, MALE, 38

I divide my money into four separate envelopes in my pocketbook. It makes me feel like I have a lot of money.

NURSE, FEMALE, 39

My boyfriend keeps track of every penny, and I mean every penny, he spends. During the course of the day, he'll make entries in a special journal he carries with him for this purpose: restaurant—$41.00, transportation—$1.50. He can go back ten years and tell you how much money he spent on liquor. Everyone thinks he's cheap because he's constantly adding.

Her boyfriend: It's a great way of budgeting and managing cash-flow. Plus I know what my net position is at any point in time. I can also tell you how much money I owe.

SECURITY ANALYST, FEMALE, 26
HER BOYFRIEND IS AN INVESTMENT BANKER, 28

I think I have a fetish about small change. I keep one new shiny quarter, one new shiny dime, one new shiny nickel and one new shiny penny, which I try never to spend, in one corner of my purse. I thought it up and I've just stuck with it for seven years now.

FORMER JOURNALIST, FEMALE, 50s

Whenever I get money from somebody, I always have to straighten out the corners and get all the nasty little folds out of it.

ACCOUNTANT, MALE, 22

Every night I divide my nickels, dimes, quarters and pennies in four cans. At the end of the month I usually have from two hundred to two hundred and fifty dollars worth of change. I go out and either buy myself something or do something stupid with it.

MARKETING MANAGER, MALE, 38

I buy things in even amounts. I'll buy $10.00 worth of gas as opposed to five gallons which may come to $8.95. When I buy clothes, I'll buy a $250 suit rather than one for $199 even if I like the uneven, lower-priced one better. In a bakery, if an item is $1.00 per pound, I'll buy it no matter what it is instead of something that may be $1.79 per pound.

VICE PRESIDENT, TELEVISION NETWORK, MALE, 30

I can't stand to be in the house with loose change in my pockets. The minute I get home, I have to empty my pockets.

DENTIST, MALE, 52

When I get paid, it must be in crisp, fresh bills. If it's dirty, I run from teller to teller until I get all new bills. Sometimes I even go to three banks in one day to get new bills. If I'm handed dirty money in change somewhere, I give it to my wife. Show her my clean money, Joan.

EXECUTIVE, TEXTILE BUSINESS, MALE, 37

I keep my bills arranged so the presidential heads are facing each other and the tails are facing each other. I'm less apt to accidentally pull two out at the same time and mistakenly pass them for one.

COMPUTER CONSULTANT, MALE, 36

I always walk with my head down looking for change. I find them all the time and it makes me very happy. Usually I find pennies but when I find a dime, I'm deliriously happy and feel like celebrating. I pick them up with a tissue, wrap them in the tissue and put it in my pocket until I get home. Then I wash them off with soap and water before I put them in my wallet.

RETIRED FORMER MODEL, FEMALE, 70s

My aunt flicks each bill about five times to make sure that she's only handing over one—even if it's to my uncle.

STUDENT, MALE, 17
HIS AUNT IS A BOOKKEEPER, 45

Every time I cash my paycheck, I smell each bill before putting it in my wallet.

JR: *Do they smell good?*

Only the new ones.

LIBRARIAN, MALE, 23

Sometimes I'll take a hundred-dollar bill and put it in the refrigerator next to the bottle of ketchup. When I open the refrigerator at seven o'clock in the morning, the first thing I see is the hundred-dollar bill. I have a feeling that it's possible to train yourself to increase your prosperity consciousness by getting used to seeing large sums of money in very common, ordinary places. I've taken a wad of money and thrown it up in the air, letting it fall all over the floor. I've put it on shelves and just let it sit there. After a while, I get used to seeing it and I expect to see money everywhere.

NUMEROLOGIST, MALE, 36

I never cut the price tags off my rugs or wall hangings. Someone told me it was probably because I don't want the feeling of permanence and if I don't cut them off, it means I can move at any time.

ACCOUNTANT, MALE, 35

The tail side of a coin has always been luckier for me. It's what I call when someone flips a coin. When I put change on a table or dresser, I turn all the coins tail side up.

SYSTEMS ANALYST, MALE, 33

I always make out a check for whole dollars and pay the cents in cash. If a bill is $35.10, then I'll make out the check for $35.00 and hand over the ten cents—it makes my checkbook so much easier to balance.

DESIGNER OF CHINA AND CRYSTAL, FEMALE, 24

If I find myself stuck with a foreign coin like a Canadian penny, I plot how to get rid of it. My conscience won't let me stick someone else directly with it even though someone stuck me with it. If a bill is $1.01, I would never pay with a dollar bill and the Canadian penny—that would be too obvious and I would be concerned that my transgression would be noticed. Most of the time I will sneak it in with some other change and hope that I get away with it.

CFO, INTERNET COMPANY, FEMALE, 39

I staple groups of money together and label them so I can keep track of them. More specifically, if I have forty dollars in my wallet and I withdraw another hundred dollars from the bank, that hundred dollars would be stapled together, labeled and set aside until the forty dollars are gone.

FILM DIRECTOR, MOTION PICTURES, MALE, 31

When the first customer of the morning hands me my fare, I spit on the first coin or bill for good luck. I acquired this habit from a former boss of mine.

CABDRIVER, MALE, 58

If I drop a nickel, dime or quarter, I'll bend down to pick it up. If I drop a penny, I don't bother. I just leave it and walk away.

HAIRDRESSER, MALE, 31

66 Instead of just tossing my change on the dresser at night, I stack it neatly in a conical shape, with the largest coin on the bottom, and the smallest on top. If anyone knocks over my change, I get very upset and I have to stack it up again. 99

TRAFFIC COORDINATOR, AD AGENCY, MALE, 22

When I first met my friend I thought she was a very open person because she would tell me absolutely everything about her sex life in gory detail. But it took me years to find out how much money she made for a living. *That* she refused to divulge.

JR: *Is her salary as good as her sex life?*

No.

SOCIAL WORKER, FEMALE, 36
HER FRIEND IS A SECRETARY, 29

I know exactly how much money, to the penny, I have on me at any given time and I know where my money is in my pockets.

JR: *Can I test you? How much do you have on you?*

I have a twenty, a ten, four singles, two quarters, a dime, three nickels and six pennies.

JR: *He showed it to me and that's exactly what he had.*

PHOTOGRAPHER, MALE, 62

God and I have a deal going. When He does something good for me, I do something good for Him. For example, I wanted to sell my car, so I told Him I'd put twenty dollars in the collection plate if I sold it. When I found a buyer, I followed through on my promise. I'm happy, He's happy—it's a wonderful system.

COURT OFFICER, MALE, 26

As far as money is concerned, I'll go to extraordinary lengths not to accumulate pennies in my change. If I go to a store and something costs $1.06, I'll give the cashier $1.11 so I'll get back one coin, a nickel, instead of giving her $1.10 and getting back four pennies in change. I just don't like to have that many objects to worry about.

MARKETING MANAGER, CORPORATION, MALE, 27

It's very difficult for me to buy something that is not on sale. If two items are the same price, I'll buy the one that's been reduced rather than the one that's straight priced. I'd almost go so far as to say that if I liked the straight priced one a little more, I'd buy the reduced one anyway.

SALES REP, ADVERTISING SPACE, FEMALE, 35

I keep the smaller-denomination bills wrapped around the outside of the larger ones so it looks as if I have less money than I do. If I'm peeling money off, I'm peeling dollar bills off and it looks less ostentatious.

ATTORNEY, PENSION INSURANCE AND TAX, MALE, "ALMOST 35"

Sometimes when I'm feeling wild and I get a cable or phone bill and the total has cents due, for example $38.56, I'll make out the check for $39.00. They just credit the amount so I'll have a 44¢ credit the next time.

STOCK ANALYST, MALE, 37

I have about twenty different bank accounts. I deposit checks from various sources in separate accounts. It's my way of keeping the books. I always know exactly how much money I've received from each particular source. And I would never use money from one source to pay another. I don't mix money.

EXECUTIVE, RETAILING, FEMALE, 46

Every day I just take a quarter, a dime, a nickel and five pennies and put it in my right pocket before I leave the house. I'm always ready to make change. Sometimes I use it and sometime I don't. If I use it then I have to replenish it so I'm ready for the next day.

GRAPHIC DESIGNER, MALE, 52

❝I'm a superstitious gambler. If I go to the track or play cards or gamble in any form, I must first discard all my pennies even if it means throwing them in the street. It's bad luck to have pennies when I gamble.**❞**

CONSTRUCTION SUPERINTENDENT, MALE, 50

When I have to remember something, a device that I developed is to hold a coin in my hand. If I have to remember one thing, I hold one coin. If I have to remember two things, I hold two coins.

PRINTER, MALE, 36

Invariably, whenever I ride the bus, at least one person, or frequently several people, will board who don't have enough change or who only have bills which the machine won't accept. For about a year now, I've been stopping at the bank every couple of days to get a roll of quarters so I have them available to help some flustered person who might otherwise have to disembark, find a place to get change and possibly be late. They're always very grateful and it makes me feel good.

RECEPTIONIST, FEMALE, 57

Any change that I have left at the end of the day goes into a little cup. Periodically, I buy myself flowers with it and that's the only thing I'll permit myself to use it for.

NURSE, FEMALE, 34

SCORE

There's more to money than spending it, saving it, earning it and worrying about it. Are you as creative managing your finances as these pros?

From zero to five similar: You're bearish on bread quirks. Spend some time studying these.

From six to ten: Count your blessings, you're average.

Over ten: You're a millionaire in quirks. Skip this chapter, you can't afford any more. Perhaps you should invest in some intensive psychotherapy.

“ If I'm having dessert and a cup of coffee, I'll put Sweet 'n Low in the coffee. Psychologically, I think I'm losing weight by saving calories even though I may be having a very caloric piece of pie. ”

EXECUTIVE, MALE, 28

Out to Lunch

In this chapter you'll find everything from soup to nuts, mostly nuts.

Remember that girl you went out with who kept blowing her nose through the entire dinner. Wasn't that the best filet mignon you never ate? But then again, didn't she look at you a little strangely when you put some of the Ajax you brought with you into your glass of water and washed all your silverware? That was after you used your napkin to wipe your chair. Clearly, you are both suffering from classic, aberrational, gastronomical behavior. Or, in short, a culinary quirk. Other symptoms are:

1. Ordering peach melba as an appetizer.
2. Eating creamed spinach with your hands.
3. Keeping your laundry in the refrigerator.
4. Having spaghetti and meatballs for breakfast.

There is no known cure for these, but don't go bananas. Your shrink is probably out to lunch too, so forget about going there for help. If you find that any of the above applies to you, here's what you can do in each situation:

1. Order matzo ball soup for dessert.
2. Sign up for a lifetime course with Amy Vanderbilt.
3. Don't invite me for dinner.
4. Wake up at 5:00 P.M.

It also helps to associate with people who can really appreciate your individual style. If you like to eat off of someone else's plate, find someone who enjoys eating off of yours. You love the egg white but hate the yellow? No problem. There are plenty of yokels around. Your quirk is that you're looking for an author with a good appetite to prepare a daily perfect gourmet dinner for after she comes home from a hard day's work? Very interesting. I can really appreciate your individual style.

Anyway, bon appetit.

I once had a girlfriend who would only eat seven string beans. She would give me a whole heap of string beans, but on her plate there were only seven. I used to call her *Seven–String Bean Mary.*

ART DIRECTOR, MALE, 39
HIS EX-GIRLFRIEND IS A GRAPHIC DESIGNER, 29

I pick up the groceries in the supermarket in the order that they're written on my list. If the bread and the cereal are next to each other in the same aisle but not one after the other on my list, I will bypass the cereal and come back for it later when I reach it on my list. Grocery shopping is like therapy for me. It's relaxing, I enjoy it, and I take my time with it.

ACTRESS, 28

Mallomars. First I eat off the chocolate top, then the marshmallow and then the cracker part. Never, *ever* would I bite into the whole thing at once. It would be obscene!

FURRIER, MALE, 50

Each time I take a bite of my meal, I have to have a little bit of every item that's on my plate on the fork. For example, if dinner consists of meat, rice and broccoli, I'll put a little bit of the meat, some rice and a little broccoli on the fork each time I take a bite throughout dinner.

STUDENT, MALE, 20

I don't like to hear people eat. If you and I were in a room together and you started to eat an apple, I'd tell you to stop or I would leave. In a restaurant there's so much noise, it doesn't matter. But if there's silence and the silence is broken by the sound of someone eating, I find it disturbing.

SALESMAN, 45

66 It's very hard for me to go to a restaurant and not taste everyone else's dish at my table. And I usually sample theirs before I try my own. 99

ACTRESS, 41

I iron my lunch every once in a while. If I want to have a quick healthy meal without doing a lot of cooking, I put mushrooms, tomatoes, lettuce and cheese in a pita bread, tuck the ends in, wrap it in aluminum foil and iron both sides for four or five minutes. The cheese melts, the bread is nice and warm and I have a delicious sandwich.

PHOTOGRAPHER, MALE, 43

I bite off the ends of hot dogs and throw them out before I eat them. I just don't like the look of them. I do the same with pickles.

ASSISTANT TELEVISION PRODUCER, MALE, 36

If I'm eating alone, I must either read or watch television. I can't just eat. I've got to have something to occupy my mind.

PACKAGING BROKER, MALE, 45

When I eat a piece of cake or something fattening, I'll take a few bites and then I'll pour salt all over it so I won't be able to finish it. I call this method *The Destroy Diet*. Sometimes in desperation I try to find an unsalted spot so I can have a bit more.

COPYWRITER, FEMALE, 41

My girlfriend will insist on using the same tea bag for her husband's cup of tea as well as her own although I would be willing, naturally, to give each of them their own tea bag.

DENTAL HYGIENIST, FEMALE, 32

I proportion each item on my plate so that if I don't complete something, there is an equal amount of each item left. My father eats the same way.

STEWARDESS, 25

I don't like to eat on Friday nights because I like to be thin going into the weekend.

HOUSEPLANT BROKER, MALE, 34

My husband cannot sit down to any meal without adjusting the lighting. They're on dimmers and it usually takes him between five and ten minutes to play around with them. He'll sit down, start to eat, he'll decide that it's too bright, get up, dim them, sit down for a while, then he may feel that it's too dark, so he'll get up again to change the intensity.

TEACHER, SEX EDUCATION, FEMALE, 35
HER HUSBAND IS AN INDUSTRIAL DESIGNER, 36

I never let anybody, including my wife, wash my beer glass with soap, only salt water. The beer tastes better!

ELEVATOR CONSTRUCTOR, MALE, 52

I like to eat food with my hands as much as possible. I especially like squishing mashed potatoes and ice cream. A couple of months ago, I broke a hand and it was fantastic having a legitimate excuse to eat that way in public and not be civilized in the least.

GARDENER, FEMALE, 25

This is an old meshugaas of mine. I prefer stale bread to fresh bread because I eat less of it. There's always a big selection of old bread in the house and I always eat the oldest one. In fact, sometimes we throw away the newer bread!

MANAGER, TIRE FACTORY, MALE, 58

I can't eat with my eyeglasses on. The food looks too clear with them, I have to eat blurry.

HOUSEWIFE, 33

66 On Monday nights, I have a card game and there's no time to cook or eat out. I have an arrangement with the owner of a deli to hold a porterhouse steak for me, which he double-wraps in aluminum foil. I place it on the block where the carburetor is—there's a spot there where it won't fall out—and by the time I get to my card game, it's perfectly done on both sides and I have a delicious dinner. 99

PHOTOGRAPHER, MALE, 43

I set a formal breakfast table for myself at night before I go to sleep. I cover the table with a tablecloth and place a complete setting for one on the table. I like to see my table set when I get up in the morning.

EXECUTIVE SECRETARY, FEMALE, 50s

I eat everything on my plate in order of preference, starting with my least favorite food and finishing with what I like best. Also, I completely finish one item before continuing on to the next. So, if there are two vegetables and meat on the plate, I'll eat one vegetable, then the other vegetable and then the meat, my favorite, last.

DENTAL TECHNICIAN, MALE, 55

My brother peels everything from a tomato to a grape. He won't eat them otherwise.

SALES ENGINEER, MALE, 53
HIS BROTHER IS A BUSINESSMAN, 47

My wife, Miriam, thinks that everything always tastes better off of my plate than off of hers. That way, it looks like she's eating like a bird!

ATTORNEY, MALE, 32
MIRIAM IS A SPEECH PATHOLOGIST, 30

I rotate my dishes, silverware and glasses so they all wear evenly. More specifically, I have a service for eight and if three of them are washed and five are left in the cabinet, I can't take the three that are clean and put them on top of the pile. I have to put them at the bottom of the pile so that I'm not using the same three plates over and over again. It's the same for the silverware. I put the ones that are cleanly washed underneath so the old ones come up to the top. I suppose that way they don't feel that I'm ignoring some of them!

ADMINISTRATOR, TELEVISION, MALE, 29

If there's one last bit of food left on a dish or tray, the last olive, or carrot, or piece of bread, I won't have it because it's bad luck. I also won't purchase the last item left on a supermarket shelf for the same reason.

TEXTILE WHOLESALER, MALE, 33

Sometimes I eat before I go out to dinner with a date so I won't be famished and make a pig of myself.

VOCATIONAL REHABILITATION COUNSELOR, FEMALE, 29

When I was little, we had an argument about whether we should eat the vegetables or meat or the things we liked or disliked first. So I began eating my food in alphabetical order. You have to know how to spell, though.

BANKER, MALE, 26

When my boyfriend cooks, we cannot sit down to eat until all the pots and any dishes or utensils in the sink have been washed. As a result, we very often have a cold hot meal.

VETERINARIAN, FEMALE, 36
HER BOYFRIEND IS A BUILDER, 41

When a friend of mine eats meat and potatoes and peas, she has one pea with every forkful of potatoes and meat. If she runs out of peas, she won't finish her meal no matter how much food is left.

HOUSEWIFE, EARLY 50s
HER FRIEND IS A REAL ESTATE AGENT, 51

I eat everything on my plate—the meat, the potatoes, the vegetables, and sometimes the salad—evenly, in rotation, so I'm finished with everything at the same time.

VICE PRESIDENT, TELEVISION NETWORK, MALE, 49

“ Whether I'm having an elaborate meal or just an Oreo cookie, I like to eat by candlelight. **”**

NATIONAL MANAGER, BREWERY, MALE, 50s

When I'm slicing up something like bananas or carrots, I have to eat the last piece. I've tried not to but it still ends up in my mouth!

CHARTIST, FEMALE, "30-PLUS"

I feel guilty eating a whole piece of cake so I play a game with myself by going back and forth into the refrigerator and cutting very small slivers. I usually finish the whole thing anyway and end up feeling guilty.

SOCIAL WORKER, FEMALE, 33

My husband doesn't like the different items of food on his plate to touch so he eats off an old steel army plate that has sections. He feels that if one food touches the other, they're both contaminated—they're supposed to be two separate foods and they no longer are if they touch.

HOUSEWIFE, 32
HER HUSBAND IS A NATIONAL SALES MANAGER, CORPORATION, 30

I mix all the food on my plate together. Everything I eat is a casserole or becomes one when it's put in front of me. It all merges together in the end anyway.

ART DIRECTOR, MALE, 30

I know it's silly because they don't taste any different, but I separate my M&M's by color before I eat them. Usually there are more of some colors than others so I eat all the extra ones until there are an even number of each color left and then I eat each color one at a time until they're all gone. I save the green M&M's for last because those are the prettiest. I eat the brown ones first because I like those the least, then the light browns. I get rid of the oranges next, then the yellows, and finally the greens.

FINANCIAL ANALYST, FEMALE, 32

PEOPLE DO THE DARNDEST THINGS!

I absolutely cannot eat a Bavarian cream puff without saying "Mmmmmmmmmmmmmmm, mmmmmmmmmmmmmmm, San Antone!" I've tried not to but the minute I put a bite in my mouth, I hear myself saying, "Mmmmmmmmmmmmmm, mmmmmmmmmmmmmmmmm, San Antone!" It's physically impossible not to!

ILLUSTRATOR, MALE, 42

My life is spent at lunch with clients and I'm supposed to act extremely sophisticated. Unfortunately, I have two obnoxious habits which I do without thinking, even in the most elegant restaurants. One is crunching ice. When one has lunch with presidents and vice presidents of client companies, and one orders a spritzer, one should not sit there and crunch ice. Crunching ice is bad enough, but the other annoying thing I generally do, again without thinking, is chew straws until I absolutely mangle them.

ACCOUNT EXECUTIVE, AD AGENCY, MALE, 29

I take vitamins by increasing size to allow my throat to adjust to the larger size.

INVESTIGATOR, INSURANCE COMPANY, MALE, 32

I line up the vitamin bottles on the kitchen counter from the tallest to the smallest. I take them in that sequence, the largest on down.

HAIRSTYLIST, MALE, 35

I take a lot of vitamins in the morning and I always swallow them in alphabetical order according to the letter of the vitamin. I start with vitamin B-1, then I take vitamin C. Next I take vitamin D, which I take before vitamin E, and then I take the multiple last.

WRITER, TELEVISION, MALE, 28

Every couple of weeks, I cook dinner in my dishwasher. I put potatoes, onions, carrots, a piece of fish or little pieces of beef and about two inches of water in a large pot with a screw-on lid. I put it in the dishwasher, run it through the cycle, without soap, of course, and I have a perfectly steamed, nutritious meal when I take it out.

PHOTOGRAPHER, MALE, 43

I eat the bun and throw the hamburger away. I don't like the idea of eating meat but I like the flavor. So when I go to a fast-food restaurant like Burger King, I order the hamburger but all I eat is the lettuce and tomato and the bread which has the flavor of the meat. I do the same with apples. I eat the peel, which has more vitamins anyway, and throw the apple away. I always pick out the best parts of food when I'm eating and throw the rest away. That's the way I am with life. I feel a little uncomfortable about doing it in public but I have friends now who just accept it as part of me so it's no big deal anymore.

MANAGER, BOUTIQUE, FEMALE, 22

I always peel a banana very well, taking all the little skins off. Then I put it under running cold water and dry it off before I eat it. I'm not a clean nut—it has nothing to do with germs. It just seems to taste fresher somehow.

EXECUTIVE SECRETARY, FEMALE, 33

I cut my spaghetti with a knife and fork in neat bite-sized chunks. I start at the front of the plate and work my way to the back. I don't like to deal with the winding.

His wife: He even did it in Italy and offended a lot of Italians!

HOUSE PAINTER, MALE, 38

I keep going back to a restaurant until I've sampled everything on the menu at least once. To break the monotony, I do three or four restaurants at one time. Then I'll start going to a different one.

SALES AGENT, ACCESSORIES, MALE, 46

I used to work for a real character who ate the exact same lunch every single day of his life—liverwurst on rye. And every day he would comment, "This liverwurst is so thin, you can read a newspaper through it."

COMMERCIAL PHOTOGRAPHER, MALE, 48
HIS FORMER EMPLOYER IS A RETIRED ART DEALER, MALE, 70s

If you'd come into the kitchen while I'm cooking, you'd see forks, spoons, utensils, plates and pots all over. If I'm mixing the peas, I'll use one spoon; if I'm making a sauce, I'll use another spoon or fork. If you'd come into the kitchen while George was cooking, you'd see one solitary utensil, a fork or spoon which he uses for everything. He eats with the same fork he cooks with. He uses the same plate for all his food. It's going into the same stomach, he reasons, so he might as well put it on the same plate. George is the kind of guy who doesn't like to waste things. You'd never see him throw away a piece of paper that doesn't have every space completely filled. On the other hand, I hardly write anything on a piece of paper before I throw it out. What's interesting is that we live together very well and we have such opposite habits.

PSYCHOTHERAPIST, FEMALE, 38
GEORGE IS A MANUFACTURER OF HANDBAGS, 48

I take the kernels of corn off the cob with a fork as opposed to eating it right off the cob. It's neater and more convenient than biting it off. I once saw an uncle of mine do it who had trouble with his false teeth and I thought it was a fabulous idea.

PRODUCTION MANAGER, PRINTING COMPANY, MALE, 44

❝ I eat five or six bananas every day on my way to work in a three-piece suit."

His girlfriend: "He puts the peels in a bag and just keeps eating them. If he can't get them in one shop, he goes to another shop or sidewalk vendor along his route until he finds them. **❞**

BANKER, MALE, 26
HIS GIRLFRIEND IS A GRADUATE STUDENT, 24

My father eats a banana sideways, like corn on the cob. He eats them in sections.

Her father: There are four natural sections to a banana—four major breaking points—and I try to eat it by each individual section.

STUDENT, FEMALE, 20
HER FATHER IS A MANUFACTURER'S REPRESENTATIVE, 49

I never put my coffee cup back in the saucer after I take the first sip. I tend to put it on the counter or table. A friend of mine pointed this out to me about six years ago. I never realized it until then.

PHYSICIAN, MALE, 35

The meat and the vegetables must be in separate dishes because I can't stand the thought of the juices running into each other.

TEACHER, JUNIOR HIGH SCHOOL, FEMALE, 26

I start off eating corn from the left side and I go down and around and then move to the right a little bit and I keep doing that until it's done or I don't want any more. This way if I don't want a whole ear of corn, maybe only half, I can cut it and give an entire untouched half to my girlfriend who promptly makes a mess of it.

MANAGEMENT CONSULTANT, MALE, 55

I have a habit of eating my desserts first because it's the best part of the meal. I don't want the restaurant to run out of my favorite dessert or my stomach to run out of room.

SECRETARY, FEMALE, WOULD NOT GIVE AGE

When I eat my cereal, I prefer not to see the spoon full of milk. I pour the milk off each spoonful, eat the cereal, and at the end I'm left with a bowl of milk.

ARCHITECT, MALE, 29

I always drink coffee or tea out of a stemmed glass. I don't like it out of a cup. No matter how highly glazed it is, china or porcelain is still porous and absorbs a little of whatever was left in it last, despite how much you wash it.

ASSISTANT TELEVISION PRODUCER, MALE, 36

My husband loves fruit and eats lots of it—plums, pears, oranges—he eats three Granny Smith apples every night. They all have these little stickers on them. When he has a piece of fruit he peels off the little sticker and sticks it on the edge of the sink. Every day practically the entire width of the sink is decorated with these stickers. He will not put them in the trash can—he likes sticking it on the edge of the sink. I've asked him why but he doesn't have an explanation. It drives me crazy because I'm the one who has to peel them off the sink and put them in the trash can. Sometimes it doesn't quite make it into the trash can and then it ends up on the bottom of my shoe or somewhere else in the house. There are apple stickers everywhere in the house. But if this is the only complaint about my marriage—then it must be pretty good!

LIBRARIAN, FEMALE, 30
HER HUSBAND IS THE DIRECTOR OF A NOT-FOR-PROFIT ORGANIZATION, 31

When I eat an ear of sweet corn, I butter, salt and eat three rows at a time. It always seemed logical—you don't get your fingers as sloppy. Consequently, it's very nice if the corn works out to have twelve or fifteen rows.

AIRLINE PILOT, MALE, 43

Most people hold the knife in their right hand and the fork in the left. I do the reverse and always have. I hold the fork in my right hand and the knife in my left and I eat in this fashion, although I'm right-handed.

ARTIST, MALE, 32

"I like to make dirty words with the letters in Campbell's soup. Sometimes I put them on a cracker. I won't say them in public and it gives me a kick to do it through my soup.**"**

ACCOUNTANT, MALE, 22

I keep important papers and documents, like my dissertation, in the vegetable compartment of the refrigerator because it's the most fire-proof place in my apartment.

ANTHROPOLOGIST, FEMALE, 31

I can't eat food that's two different textures. For instance, I can't eat a tomato because it's hard on the outside and squishy on the inside. It gives me a violent reaction. You bite through the hard part and it squishes all over the inside of your mouth and to me, that's disgusting.

GRADUATE STUDENT, MALE, 26

I always eat three french fries at a time. I don't know why—I just have to do it. If I get to the end and there's only one or two left, I'll throw them out—absolutely—I swear. It's the weirdest thing. Anyone who sits with me actually takes note of it.

PROGRAMMER, MALE, 25

I look in people's refrigerators when I visit them because you can learn a lot about people this way. In fact, last night I was at my neighbor's house and I looked in her refrigerator. I apologized before I did it but I did it anyway. And I was very impressed. She had all natural eggs and hormone-free nonfat skim milk. It shows that she's aware about antibiotics and the environment but, incredibly, she had Wonder bread. *Wonder bread!*—I couldn't believe it! Despite the Wonder bread, I'll still associate with her because she's nice.

TELEVISION FILM DIRECTOR, MALE, 39

Our daughter never finishes a meal completely no matter how hungry she is. She'll leave one bite of each item on her plate.

CONFEREE, MALE, 47
HIS DAUGHTER IS A DENTAL HYGIENIST, 22

I eat pie Continental style. Instead of eating from the point to the back, I start from the back where the crust is and work my way forward. I like the taste of the crust first instead of leaving it for last.

ADVERTISING COORDINATOR, MALE, 23

We have plenty of regular cups and glasses but I've adopted a little fruit jar as my water glass. This quirk originated in the navy and it just stuck with me.

MAINTENANCE MAN, 60

Instead of buying plastic utensils and condiments like sugar, salt, Sweet 'n Low, soy sauce, or ketchup, I just take some packets from coffee or take-out places. I save a lot of money this way.

ADMINISTRATIVE ASSISTANT, FOREIGN MISSION, FEMALE, 24

I chew on chicken bones to make myself feel like I've eaten something when I haven't. I enjoy chewing on them. In fact, I usually take the meat off the bones and eat the bones.

REMEDIAL MATH TEACHER, FEMALE, 29

I sit on the same chair at the counter in my home to eat my meals. There are four chairs at the counter and I always seem to take the one on the right.

JR: *If it's taken, are you upset?*

Yes, if one of my kids is sitting in it, I'll ask them to move.

BOND SALESMAN, 47

My father has to end a meal by taking one bite of each item on his plate. If any food is not completely finished, he leaves it over. He calls it a *Balanced Meal*.

STYLIST, FEMALE, 23
HER FATHER IS AN ARCHITECT, 54

❝ I bring lots of food with me to the movies because the minute I sit down, I get hungry. I prefer sandwiches or chicken to popcorn or candy. It makes the movie more enjoyable. I bring some wet paper towels with me so I can wipe my hands. ❞

MAID, FEMALE, 60

QUEASY CUISINE

My mother always got involved in some very strange sandwiches. First, because she's from the Deep South, and second, because she grew up during the depression. She's been known to eat pineapple and mayonnaise sandwiches, usually on white bread. And often she'll take a can of Campbell's bean soup and spread it on bread and eat that as a sandwich.

MARKETING CONSULTANT, FEMALE, 53
HER MOTHER IS A HOUSEWIFE, 74

I like to eat condiments—soy sauce, mayonnaise, mustard, tartar sauce, salad dressing. I'll go into the refrigerator with a spoon and eat a little bit of each one.

FINANCIAL ANALYST, FEMALE, 25

My grandfather struck me as being peculiar when I went to visit my grandparents one summer in Kansas City. We were having breakfast and my grandmother pulled a pot off the stove and served him chicken gravy on his pancakes. I couldn't believe it. But he grew up on a farm in Kansas and apparently they didn't have maple syrup there.

LIBRARY RESEARCHER, MALE, 26

When I eat any kind of sandwich, I put mayonnaise on one side and mustard on the other.

HACK DRIVER, OWNS HORSE AND CARRIAGE, MALE, 24

I eat potato chip sandwiches. Potato chips on white bread. I don't put anything else on it. It's a very simple sandwich and it's delicious! When I'm really hungry, that's what I think about.

HAIR COLORIST, MALE, "DON'T ASK MY AGE—
I'LL HAVE A NERVOUS BREAKDOWN"

I love mayonnaise sandwiches on white bread at any time.

PHARMACIST, MALE, 31

My brother's favorite food to eat in the whole world is sweet pickles and peanut butter on white bread. *Revolting!* The thought of it makes me sick. And I really can't understand it because he's a gourmet cook and a very finicky eater. But he just loves it and he's been eating it for years.

ASSISTANT ACCOUNT EXECUTIVE, FEMALE, 21
HER BROTHER IS A STUDENT, 17

I like to put applesauce on my hot dog. It started when I was pregnant twenty years ago.

ADMINISTRATIVE ASSISTANT, FEMALE, 48

My grandmother used to put orange juice on her cereal and when we asked her why she did it, she said it didn't matter, she couldn't taste it anyhow! She was 80.

TEXTILE WHOLESALER, MALE, 33

SCORE

Just for the fun of it, if you want to know how your eating oddities compare with other people's, use this as a guide:

Under fifteen similar: You're only a moderately interesting dinner guest.

From fifteen to twenty-five: You're probably a riot at smorgasbords where there are so many different kinds of food to have fetishes about.

More than twenty-five: You qualify for the coveted Julia Child Culinary Quirk Award.

66 I cannot go to sleep at home or in a hotel room or in someone else's home without first pulling the bedspread, the covers and the sheets out from being tucked in so everything is loose and free and unconfined. **99**

COPYWRITER, FEMALE, 30

Bedtime Stories You Haven't Heard Before

Your mom and dad think it's cute that you sleep with a glowing Mickey Mouse night-light because you're afraid of the dark. It's a perfectly reasonable quirk. (Don't let the fact that you're a forty-three-year-old well-respected politician and the father of three children disturb you.)

Are you a *Blanket Hogger*? Someone with an overwhelming but unconscious need to slowly and systematically wind yourself up in the blanket in the middle of the night so there is no hope for your poor half-frozen partner to retrieve even a corner.

Worse than having a *Blanket Hogger* for a spouse is having one who is a *Diagonal Sleeper*. Don't plan on getting any sleep if you're late to bed.

Your honeymoon was a big hit with both of you jockeying for the same side of the bed. No wonder Ricky and Lucy slept in twin beds. The marriage vow you took was, "I do—claim the right side for the rest of my life."

Does this mean you're suffering from severe sleeping sickness? Nah, you just have a little night shtick like the rest of us.

It's amazing the rituals we take to bed with us. I mean, really, you know you set the alarm. Why get up again for the seventh time to check it? To you, the purpose of a blanket is not to keep you warm—it's, heaven forbid, to keep your knees from touching. And a pillow is not just a wad of puff to lay your head upon. Please. That's too conservative. If you line up enough of them next to you, they can substitute for a real companion, if one is not available. Or function as a pillow barrier, to defend yourself against a partner who's a particularly active sleeper. It's also a perfect device to block your spouse's snoring, or your own, or a stray ray of light, if you place it over your head. Pillow fluffing is a popular pre-snooze ritual—it's not easy getting the goose down to make a perfect contour around your head.

If your nocturnal creativity is a bit challenged, this chapter should inspire you. Nitey nite!

I name my pillows. One is Sharon Stone and the other one is Julia Roberts.

JR: *What do you do with your pillows?*

I just hold them closely and dream on those long, cold nights when I don't have female companionship.

ASSISTANT MARKETING MANAGER, MALE, 29

When I wake up in the morning, I start counting to one hundred and tell myself that when I get to one hundred, I'll get up. I always think I counted too quickly and start over. I go through this about five or six times before I actually get up.

MANAGEMENT CONSULTANT, MALE, 33

For all my life, at least from my earliest recollection, it's been physically impossible for me to fall asleep without my navel being covered. If it's summer and I'm naked, I still have to have a part of the sheet come across my navel or I can't sleep. When I'm wearing underpants, sometimes I'll be suddenly aware that something is wrong…the waistband of my underpants is too low. When I realize it, I pull the waistband over my navel and then I can go to sleep.

PHOTOGRAPHER, MALE, 28

I always sleep with the light on. The brighter, the better. I don't like the dark. Besides sleeping with the light on, I must make love with the light on. To me it's more terrific.

CRAFTS DESIGNER/AUTHOR, FEMALE, 30

The television set must be on when I go to sleep and it burns all night long. I shut it off when I wake up in the morning. I've tried to go to sleep without it—no can do!

RETAIL BUTCHER, MALE, 40

I have to sleep with my socks on, preferably tennis socks because they keep my feet warm. That's all I wear. In the summer the air conditioner is going so I still need to have my feet warm.

MANAGER, COMPUTER CENTER, MALE, 35

About twenty-five minutes after I've gotten into bed, I'll wake up and think, "I forgot to set the alarm." I check it and, of course it's okay, so I get back into bed. In another twenty-five minutes, I wake up thinking the same thing. I go through this ritual two or three times a night before I actually believe I've set it.

FASHION BUYER, FEMALE, 30

I usually sleep on my back and put the edge of the sheet between my teeth. I don't know how it started. I've tried to analyze it and decided that the worst thing that can happen is that I'll chew a hole in the sheet!

ART DIRECTOR, MALE, 45

Every night before I get into bed, I wipe my feet off, even if I've worn socks and my feet are perfectly clean. I sit down on the bed, grab each leg by the ankle and brush my feet off with my hand.

CABANA BOY, 21

I only wear long, white nightgowns. It really bothers me to think of wearing any other color because it doesn't feel clean enough. I once had to buy a green one in an emergency because the store was out of white ones and I couldn't sleep well wearing it. Sheets and pillowcases can be in other colors although my mother only uses white bedding and that always seems the absolute cleanest. It's one of the pleasures of going home and sleeping—white nightgown, white bed.

JUNIOR ACCOUNT EXECUTIVE, FEMALE, 21

66 For five years, my bed was perpendicular to the wall. Now my apartment is being redone and the bed has been built into a platform and it is now parallel to the wall. I still sleep perpendicular to the wall across the short side of the bed. It creates too much confusion within my body to adjust to the new direction so I let my feet hang over. 99

PARTNER, COMMODITY BROKERAGE FIRM, MALE, 30

I have to have a glass of ice water on my nightstand every night by 11:20, with three cubes of ice. I can't go to sleep without it. It is a glass I do not drink from. If I want water, I go to the kitchen, even if it's the middle of the night.

RECEPTIONIST, FEMALE, 21

My sheets must be 100% cotton and they must have at least 180 threads per inch. Other sheets give me abrasions.

ATTORNEY, MALE, 34

I check every bed that's not my own, in a hotel or motel, to make sure it's not short-sheeted. If it is, I have to remake the bed, because I don't want my body to touch the mattress. Most beds are short-sheeted so you can imagine how many beds I have to remake! It was not a hit on my honeymoon!

SECRETARY, FEMALE, 48

I put my underwear under my pillow when I go to sleep. I was never consciously aware that I did this—it's second nature by now—until my wife pointed it out to me one day. She asked me why I did it so I started to think about it. *Why do I do it?* It certainly doesn't accomplish anything. I finally realized that I wasn't entirely crazy—there was a perfectly valid reason for it. It started when I was in a forced labor camp in Hungary during the war. When I got undressed to prepare to go to sleep, I put my clothing in a pile. By morning, I would discover that someone, who obviously didn't have a pair, had stolen my underwear. After this incident, I began placing them under a makeshift pillow. I got so used to doing this that I just continued the habit after the war. It's still a part of my bedtime routine, although my wife has sworn she won't steal them!

DENTAL INSTRUMENT MECHANIC, MALE, 84

If my right thigh should touch my left thigh when I'm sleeping, I would immediately wake up. I can't fall asleep if they're making contact so I use the blanket to separate my legs. Someone else's skin touching mine doesn't bother me, just my own. I guess I must be allergic to myself.

PRINTER, MALE, 40

My grandmother puts a large sheet of plastic over her pillows and headboard to protect them from scalp grease. And she sleeps on the plastic.

STUDENT, FEMALE, 23
HER GRANDMOTHER IS AN ARTIST, 78

I have difficulty going to sleep at night unless I have an extra blanket wrapped around my head covering my eyes. It's a special all-cotton, full-size thermal blanket. I don't use a pillow. I just wad up the extra part and use that as a pillow. If I visit people and I miss my blanket, I borrow a large towel.

ATTORNEY, FEMALE, 33

My roommate has a little stuffed bear that she's had since she was one. The bear's name is Brendan, named after a kid she saw once and liked. You cannot touch the bear because she'll get very flustered. If you change the position of the bear, she'll get really mad. When she wakes up in the morning, she covers the bear with the blanket so the bear won't be cold.

SALES ANALYST, FINANCIAL INFORMATION COMPANY, FEMALE, 22
HER ROOMMATE IS A LAW SCHOOL STUDENT, 22

The opening of my pillowcase has to be to my right when I'm lying on my back. Always—no matter where I am.

WRITER/PRODUCER, FEMALE, 33

66 My feet or arms cannot hang over the edge of the bed because the monsters under the bed will get them. Sometimes, I have to take a running leap from the door of the bedroom to the bed because they'll get me while I'm standing there. Many times, in the middle of the night, my leg or arm will sort of fall out and I'll immediately feel it and I'll think, 'This is ridiculous, I'm thirty-two years old, there aren't any monsters under the bed!' but I have to do it or else I can't go back to sleep again!**99**

SPECIAL ASSISTANT TO MUSEUM DIRECTOR, FEMALE, 32

All my life I slept on my stomach until I had an ulcer operation and I was forced to sleep on my back. I resolved the situation by placing the pillow on my stomach, which made me feel like I was sleeping on my stomach, and since then I always sleep that way.

OWNER, CLOTHING BOUTIQUE, MALE, 32

I do some wild, neurotic things that I think are normal. I can't sleep in the middle of beds. In a conjugal bed, when she wants to cuddle, I really can't get into it because I have to be hanging off the edge of the bed, and if she starts to cuddle, I'll wind up kissing the rug. A piece of my body has to be touching the edge. It's just more comfortable that way. I get some strange reactions and questions from pseudo-psychologists who try to figure it out like, "Whatever happened to you when you were a child?"

ACCOUNT EXECUTIVE, AD AGENCY, MALE, 29

A friend of mine has to make the bed instantly as soon as she and her husband wake up. One Sunday her husband got up to go to the bathroom, and by the time he came back, the bed was made.

TEACHER, HANDICAPPED CHILDREN, FEMALE, 32
HER FRIEND IS A STOCK REPORTER, 38

When I sleep in the nude, I put a pair of undershorts near the bed, in case there's a fire in the middle of the night. I want to be able to run outside with something on!

TEXTILE WHOLESALER, MALE, 33

When I was in college and lived in the dorm, I wanted to have all my valuables nearby when I was sleeping. So, before going to bed, I'd put my wallet, my watch, my keys and any change in my shoes. It seemed reasonable at the time except, now, seventeen years later, I still do it.

OWNER, MARKETING SALES PROMOTION COMPANY, MALE, 38

I sleep on a bare mattress so I don't have to wash the sheets.

CONSULTANT, LABOR RELATIONS, MALE, 27

It's very difficult for me to make love to a woman unless she's on my right. It just feels so much better and more comfortable when I'm on the left.

SOUND ENGINEER, MALE, 33

Quite often I wake my husband up at around 2:00 A.M. to let him know that our sons are not at home and I'm concerned. I then turn over and go back to sleep while he spends the rest of the morning hours awake, waiting for them to come home. As long as he's doing my worrying for me, I can relax.

JEWELER, FEMALE, 44

When the lights are off and my husband is just about to doze off, he'll knock twice on the headboard to keep evil spirits away. He's been doing this since childhood.

HOUSEWIFE, 39
HER HUSBAND IS AN EXECUTIVE, 44

I won't sleep on sheets that have holes in them. I don't care about pillowcases or the blanket, just the sheets. I have been known to check into a motel room and spend the first five minutes or so inspecting the sheets to make sure there are no holes in them. This leads to some very strange reactions indeed from my companions who look at me as if I'm crazy, which I probably am. In fact, when my ex-wife and I first went away for a weekend, and I went through my sheet-check routine, it was almost the first and last time we went away. Perhaps, in hindsight, it might have been a better thing. My therapist can't figure it out either.

LAWYER, MALE, 36

I must have sex every day at 6:15 P.M., after the sun goes down and before the moon comes up. That's when I enjoy it most. For me, it's like brushing my teeth—it's a must. I've buried a few husbands, I'm on my third marriage.

HOUSEWIFE, 50s

I sleep very comfortably as long as I have a pillow to put over my eyes to keep any light out. I sleep with two pillows and I like room darkeners and drapes. I don't like any light whatsoever in the bedroom. As a matter of fact, if somebody would light a match, it would wake me up.

DENTIST, MALE, 45

I admire the view from our bedroom window of the Manhattan skyline and every night before I go to sleep, I say goodnight to the Empire State Building.

His wife: When he's out of town, I do it for him. I say, "Goodnight from Marshall," with my eyes focused on the Empire State Building.

COMPUTER CONSULTANT, MALE, 36
HIS WIFE IS A STUDENT, 33

I sleep with four pillows lined up alongside myself. I make believe it's another body next to me.

INSURANCE SALESMAN, 44

No matter how great a party we've been to or how extensive a dinner we've had, my husband and I must have a bowl of cereal right before we go to sleep. If I don't have the cereal, I will think I'm famished and simply cannot get through the night.

HOUSEWIFE, 60
HER HUSBAND IS AN ENGINEER, 65

My particular quirk developed when I was in the navy. When the ships would rock, I'd feel very uncomfortable and unstable. I was always afraid I would fall off the bed, which was a cot at the time. So I developed the habit of putting one foot on the floor to fall asleep. I've been out of the service for many years but to this day, I have to sleep with one leg on the floor. I've been married a couple of times and my wives have thought this to be highly unusual. But it works.

TELEVISION PRODUCER, MALE, 39

We're married forty-one years, and for at least forty-one years, he fluffs his pillow about five times every night before he goes to sleep.

REGISTERED NURSE, FEMALE, 64
HER HUSBAND IS A PHYSICIAN, 67

After my boyfriend and I make love, he gets up and waters the plants. Sometimes it gives him energy and instead of just cooling out, he waters the plants. We have about a hundred of them.

PROGRAM AUDITOR, FEMALE, 22
HER BOYFRIEND IS A HARVARD M.B.A. CANDIDATE, 23

I like very smooth, soft pillowcases and I bring my own with me on all my trips. I use the satin acetate kind or very old ones that are almost falling apart so they're very soft. I also bring my own pillow, except, of course, when I'm traveling overseas and the weight or bulk or number of pieces of luggage is a factor. The only pillows I can sleep on are foam rubber.

TEXTILE DESIGNER, FEMALE, 34

When my husband and I go to bed every evening, he gets into bed wearing his undershorts, and I take them off. It has nothing to do with sex. He doesn't do the same for me because I go to bed nude.

SOCIAL WORKER, FEMALE, 33

" Unless I have my two pigs, I can't go to sleep at night. One is gray and female and the other one is pink and male. They're stuffed animals. I use them to prop up my elbow and knee and when I'm away from home I have to substitute with pillows, but it's just not the same. **"**

FILMMAKER, FEMALE, 28

Ever since I traveled around Europe as a student eight years ago, I've slept with my watch on. At the time, we stayed in hostels and hotels and I didn't want it to get stolen. Later I saw Jean-Paul Belmondo in a movie and he always kept his watch on, so that reinforced my quirk.

ACCOUNT EXECUTIVE, AD AGENCY, MALE, 29

I'm most comfortable when one leg is underneath the blanket and the other leg is on top. When I turn around, the leg that was under goes over, and the other leg goes under.

ART DIRECTOR, MALE, 45

I don't like going to bed and, for all intents and purposes, waking up the next second and having eight to twelve hours of my life disappear. I like to experience those hours so I get up several times during the night. I like the quiet and the solitude. I also enjoy languishing in bed and the experience of going back to sleep.

GEMOLOGIST, MALE, 27

In order to fall asleep, I must be lying so that my head is pointed toward the west and my feet are to the east. Otherwise I just can't sleep. I was once in a hotel on vacation and I had a very difficult time falling asleep, until it finally occurred to me that the bed was in the wrong direction. When I turned it around, I was immediately able to fall asleep. Since then, I always take a compass with me when I travel. As soon as I arrive in my room, I arrange the bed so that it's lined up east and west.

DENTAL INSTRUMENT MECHANIC, MALE, 84

I sleep in the nude with the window open and don't use a blanket no matter what the weather is.

SECURITY GUARD, MALE, 34

In a James Bond movie I once saw or a James Bond book that I read, the heroine said to James Bond, "James, if you sleep on your left side, it's bad for your heart. Sleep on the other side." I took that advice "to heart," and since then I always sleep on my right side. Conveniently, it also happens to be good for my marriage because I snore and the way we're arranged, that faces me away from my wife so it's a little less loud.

REDEVELOPMENT EXECUTIVE, MALE, 47

I make my bed when I get home at night even if it's only fifteen minutes before I go to sleep. I have to get into a neat bed but I can't be bothered making it in the morning. Sometimes I'll get home at eleven o'clock at night, make the bed, then unmake it, get in and go to sleep.

ATTORNEY, MALE, 26

Anything I do or come into contact with at night, right before I go to bed, I must do or touch three times. I check the locks on the door, and actually lock and unlock them three times. My alarm clock is set for seven o'clock but I go around and reset it three times. I turn the alarm on and off and make sure it rings three times. I brush my teeth three times. I rinse my face three times. I flip my pillow over three times. When I was small, I used to watch my father play cards. He would walk around his chair three times for good luck to win the game and that's probably where it originated. Three's the magic number!

HOUSEWIFE, 28

When my grandmother goes to sleep, she points one shoe forward and the other one in the opposite direction so no one can step into them at night. She's Italian.

SALES MANAGER, MALE, 35
HIS GRANDMOTHER IS 79

66 My friend and his wife usually sleep head to head but during a full moon he sleeps head to foot because he's afraid he'll wake up in the middle of the night and bite her neck. 99

MANAGER, RETAIL STORE, MALE, 32
HIS FRIEND IS A BANK VICE PRESIDENT, 35

I check the entire house to make sure that all the drawers, closets and windows are shut tight before I go to sleep, regardless of how tired I may be. If it's open just a hair, I won't be able to sleep.

FASHION BUYER, FEMALE, 30

I suffer from a chronic *Hot Feet* condition which requires me to have my feet outside the covers at all times regardless of the temperature. Until about a month ago, I was convinced that monsters were circulating in my room ready to kill me during the night—probably for good reason. The monsters and I had a pact, however, that they would not attack my feet. They could attack any other part of me but they would leave my feet alone and that way we would get along.

DEVELOPMENT COORDINATOR, PUBLIC TV STATION, MALE, 22

I must wear a fresh, clean nightgown every night. If I'm on vacation and I run out of clean ones, I'll keep washing the one I have even if I've worn it only once.

HOUSEWIFE, 58

Every night before I go to sleep, no matter where I am, I try to have milk and cookies, or milk and a cupcake. If, for some reason, it's not possible, I'm grouchy and don't feel satisfied and can't fall asleep right away. If I realize that I'm out of milk or cookies or cupcakes, I'll get dressed, go out in the middle of the night and drive as far as a mile to get some.

CAB OWNER/DRIVER, MALE, 30

Before I go to bed, I have to lift up the receiver of the telephone to make sure that I get a dial tone and it's working. I just want to be sure that I can be reached in case of an emergency.

OFFICE MANAGER FOR ORTHODONTIST, FEMALE, 52

❝ My wife, Elenore, has a special pillow that goes with her wherever she goes. It's been all over the world. She can't sleep on a strange pillow. **❞**

PRODUCE MERCHANDISING MANAGER, MALE, 47
ELENORE IS A HOUSEWIFE, 47

I always sleep with my right hand flat against the wall over my head. It doesn't matter in what position I fall asleep, I still hold the wall. I like a lot of blankets but I also like to be cool when I sleep and touching a cold wall helps to cool me down.

MARKETING MANAGER, COSMETICS COMPANY, FEMALE, 24

I must have a tissue in my hand when I go to bed in case I have to blow my nose in the middle of the night. If a facial tissue is unavailable, I'll use a piece of toilet paper or a napkin. I hold it as I fall asleep. And if I wake up during the night, I look for it or take another one if I can't find it because I usually let go of it at some point. There are always tissues tucked around my bed.

MANAGER, PRESCHOOL, FEMALE, 30

Every night, before we go to sleep, my husband and I simultaneously say a four-line poem that his mother used to say to him as a child. And occasionally, when we're apart, I say it anyway. It goes like this: Goodnight. Sleep tight. Pleasant dreams. See you in the morning.

WRITER, FEMALE, 27
HER HUSBAND IS A BANKER, 27

SCORE

Are you in the dark about your nocturnal habits? Come out from under the covers and 'fess up.

If you recognize yourself six times or less: You think you're normal? Dream on.

Seven to seventeen times: You're probably divorced—at least four times.

Over eighteen times: Consider this a wake-up call. I have a support group for you. Good luck.

66 When my husband gets dressed in the morning, he puts on his pants, zips up the zipper, buttons the button, buckles the belt, then goes and gets his shirt, unbuckles the belt, unbuttons the button, unzips the zipper, tucks in his shirt and then does it all up again. 99

HOUSEWIFE, 30
HER HUSBAND IS AN AIRLINE PILOT, 32

Clothes Encounters of the Strange Kind

Who's to tell you how to dress or undress. Billy Crystal puts his shoes on before his pants, Queen Elizabeth II uses her pocketbook to send signals to her staff and Woody Allen likes to wear sneakers with his tux, so you're in good company.

Clothes mean different things to different people. To exotic dancer Bubbles LaRose, they mean absolutely nothing. But for the rest of us—it's time to come out of the closet. You nonconformists with a pink mohawk and every body part pierced, are you listening? If God wanted you to have four earrings in each earlobe and one in your right nostril, he would have put more holes in your head. If you want to wear your shirt unbuttoned to your navel with lots of gold chains, suit yourself. If status initials are your bag, Louis Vuitton loves people like you. He's cashing in on your quirk right this minute. If you painstakingly file each item in your closet one by one, style by style, year by year, bar mitzvah by bar mitzvah—all facing in the same direction, of course—you belong here. The worst thing that can happen if you're a *Sock, Shoe, Sock, Shoe Person* as opposed to a *Sock, Sock, Shoe, Shoe Person* is that you'll hop out of your apartment if there's a fire. And if you're a *Tall Blond Man with One Black Shoe and One Brown Shoe* and it happens regularly—even on Daylight Savings mornings when you don't have a hangover—you certainly qualify.

Tomorrow morning concentrate on which leg you put in your pants or panty hose first, then try to do it the other way. Then come up with a good excuse explaining to your boss why you were late. Some people put both legs in their pants at the same time. They're unbalanced people.

Just remember that it's not whether you put your underwear on first or last that counts. It's whether they're clean—in case you get into an accident.

I always wear blue on Monday because it's the first day of the work week and as far as I'm concerned it's *Blue Monday*. Unconsciously, I wore a blue shirt and blue pants one Monday about two years ago. Someone at work—who always wears blue on Mondays, but I hadn't noticed—thought that perhaps I did too, and asked me, "Are you wearing blue for *Blue Monday*?" That concept had never occurred to me, of course, and I replied, "No, but from now on I think I will!" And sure enough, ever since then, I wear a blue shirt and blue pants every Monday; I may wear light blue on some other days of the week but on Monday I wear a really dark blue—navy blue. And, two more colleagues have also started to wear blue on Mondays. *Blue Monday*—the first day of the work week!

MECHANICAL ENGINEER, MALE, 52

If I'm wearing a T-shirt, a shirt and a sweater, when I'm ready to get undressed, I'll unbutton the top button of my shirt, and pull the entire three layers off over my head at the same time.

EXECUTIVE, MALE, 30

When I put my panty hose on, I always put my right leg in first. I've tried to do it the other way, but I have to take it off, and put it on again with my right leg first.

JR: *Why?*

If I knew why, it wouldn't be a quirk!

FUND-RAISER, FEMALE, WOULD NOT GIVE AGE

I only wear red socks. It makes my feet feel better. I like getting very dressed up in elegant clothing and wearing red socks. It's cheerful to look down and see them. I think Van Johnson always wore red socks. Otherwise, I'm a very conservative dresser.

COMMERCIAL PHOTOGRAPHER, MALE, 48

❝ When my wife gets up in the morning, before she throws her panties in the hamper, she dusts the furniture with them. When I ask her why she does it, she says, "Did I do that? I didn't even notice." **❞**

DENTAL INSTRUMENT MECHANIC, MALE, 84
HIS WIFE IS 76

I iron only the front of my shirt and the sleeves because that's all that shows when I wear a suit. If I take the jacket off, I still have the vest on. It takes too much time to iron the whole shirt.

SYSTEMS ANALYST, MALE, 23

I change my underwear at least three times a day—in the morning, when I come home from work and before I go to bed. It's a hygienic thing. Some people have to wash their hands eight hundred times a day—I just change my underwear.

ACCOUNT EXECUTIVE, PUBLIC RELATIONS, FEMALE, 27

I go nuts if all the hangers aren't facing in the same direction. The hooks must be pointed toward the back and all my clothes have to be facing the same way. If they're not, I think it looks disorderly.

PRESIDENT, AD AGENCY, MALE, 35

I like to line up my shoes under the bed, like soldiers. I have about a dozen pairs under there. My wife thinks I'm nuts. They're easier to get on this way—I just step out of bed and put on my shoes! Otherwise, I'd have to go to the closet.

RETOUCHER, MALE, 58

I like my clothes completely wrinkled. I hate anything brand-new. In fact, I scuff up a new pair of shoes before I wear them. I'll walk through mud, get them wet, walk on the sides of them. If it's already wrinkled, I don't have to worry about getting it wrinkled. I'm more comfortable and relaxed.

MODEL, MALE, 35

I put my shirt and jacket on at the same time. It's quicker.

BARTENDER, MALE, 22

I have to have one brand-new item of everything I might wear in my closet for a special occasion. I have a new pair of socks, a new pair of underwear, a new shirt, a new tie, a new pair of shoes and pajamas. I don't know exactly when I'm going to use them but when I do, I must replace them.

BLOUSE MANUFACTURER, MALE, 52

The laces in my shoes have to have equal tension. If one shoelace is looser than the other, I have to stop and retie both so the pressure is exactly the same.

ESTIMATOR, AD AGENCY MEDIA DEPARTMENT, FEMALE, 22

For years now, I've worn nothing but knee-length, black woolen socks. I never have to worry about matching them up with each other or to my suit because black will match anything.

JR: *What about in the summer?*

Same thing—calf-length, black woolen socks.

JR: *What about with a light suit?*

Still, black socks.

PUBLIC RELATIONS, MALE, MID-40s

When I want to remind myself about something, I turn my watch around and wear it with the dial underneath. It's so uncomfortable that I always remember what I have to do.

WAITER, MALE, 33

My grandmother, who was in the jewelry business, taught me never to wear white gold or silver with yellow gold. She felt it wasn't right to mix the two so I never do.

MARKETING CONSULTANT, FEMALE, 33

I put on a different cologne every day of the week. I don't like to smell the same scents on myself consistently. If I was particularly lucky one day, I'll wear the same cologne to bring me luck again when I feel I need it.

OWNER, WHOLESALE FOOD BUSINESS, MALE, 41

About ten or fifteen years ago, I noticed that a friend of mine, who has the same passion for shoes as I do, polished the soles of his shoes as well as the top. He said it made them more waterproof and they lasted longer. That made perfectly good sense to me and I've been doing the same thing ever since. He was right.

OWNER, FOREIGN TRADE COMPANY, MALE, 40

In order to put my socks on, I have to sit down and while I'm sitting it makes good sense to put my shoes on. Then I put my pants on. Otherwise, after I sit down to put my socks on I would have to stand up to put my pants on and then sit down again to put my shoes on.

JR: *Why don't you put on your pants and then sit down and put your socks and shoes on?*

Because I wear socks that come all the way up to my knees.

JR: *You can roll up your pants.*

That's too complicated.

CONTROLLER, MALE, 48

It drives me nuts to see people walking around with their pocket flaps in or their collar up. I have to go over and say, "Why don't you fix your pocket flaps, you'll get wrinkles." They do adjust their pocket or collar but their expression says, "Who are you? Why do you care?"

RETOUCHER, MALE, 26

I keep lists of the garments I wear during the week so I don't repeat them right away. If I notice on my list that I wore a particular outfit last Monday, I'll wait another week before I wear it again.

FASHION DESIGNER, FEMALE, 31

I don't use an ironing board even if there's one in the house. It's so much easier to put a towel on the bed and iron on the bed, especially since I iron my clothes the day I'm going to wear them, not all at the same time.

ADMINISTRATIVE ASSISTANT, FEMALE, 24

A lot of people are fascinated by the fact that I wear a white sock on my left foot and another color, which changes from day to day, on my right foot. I like to be unique.

LADIES' APPAREL MANUFACTURER, MALE, 44

I never, ever wear my underpants right side out. I always wear them inside out to keep the little label from rubbing and chafing the small of my back.

COPYWRITER, MALE, 37

I always wear my watch on my right hand. The number of right-handed people who wear their watch on their right hand is about one in every ten million. It feels hideously uncomfortable on the left hand.

MUSICIAN, MALE, 37

I've always felt that I can run faster and feel much lighter with something white on my feet, so I always wear white socks and white sneakers when I participate in sports.

ORTHODONTIST, MALE, 41

66 My parents' neighbor in suburbia wears a different outfit for every chore around the house. He has a Garage Attendant outfit for fixing the car. He has a Gardener outfit for landscaping. He has a Painter outfit for painting. He has a Chef outfit for cooking. He's very serious about this. I was up there visiting one time and I said to my father, 'The guy next door must have hired a garage attendant to come fix his car.' And my father said, 'No, that's him.' 🙯

WRITER, FEMALE, 36
HER PARENTS' NEIGH-
BOR IS A DENTIST, 45

There are two types of socks—regular, which are worn during the day, and *Sleep-O's*, which are worn to bed. When a regular sock is used up, I make a *Sleep-O* out of it by making the necessary alterations. You can't just go out and buy a pair of *Sleep-O's*. *Sleep-O's* are made not born. It's very important that they have enough give around the ankles so that it doesn't affect the circulation. They should also have a hole in the heel for air and be slightly damp at the toes to relax the calf muscles. By morning half the sock is off so the heel is exposed and only the toes are covered. I wear them as a protective covering because I can't stand the feeling of the sheets against my toes.

EXECUTIVE, MALE, 44

I never take jewelry off unless it breaks off. I wash my hands and take a shower with my rings and necklaces.

SHOWROOM SALESWOMAN, 25

When I buy a pair of shoes, I only try on one. I assume the other one will fit. No matter what, I keep them. I expect shoes to hurt.

INVESTMENT BANKER, MALE, 34

My closet is filled with size eight clothing although I'm a size fourteen. I just can't bring myself to buy such a large size because I was once a size eight and I keep thinking that if I buy beautiful things in a small size it will be incentive to lose weight. So far I haven't and I'm running out of things to wear.

HOUSEWIFE, 53

I will never again wear an outfit that I wore to a funeral or in which I had a bad experience.

HOUSEWIFE, 35

I can't stand the thought of being seen in white underwear and black socks. I think it's almost as bad as wearing white socks with black shoes and pants. It just doesn't work. If I'm getting undressed, I make sure to take my socks off first or if I'm getting dressed, I do so in such an order that I can't be seen with just white underwear and black socks.

STUDENT, MALE, 25

I never wear underwear or an undershirt during the day but I do sleep in them just in case there's a fire. Or, if a robber breaks in, I don't want to have to go chasing after him balls-ass naked. Also sexually it's great to have underwear on.

TATTOO ARTIST, MALE, 35

My mother has a batch of clothes for every season. As the seasons change, she brings down the new batch from the attic and wears them exactly in order. She does not select clothes according to her mood, she wears whatever is next in line so she doesn't have to think about her clothes.

ASSISTANT BUYER, FEMALE, 24
HER MOTHER IS A HOUSEWIFE, 55

I change at least five times before I leave the house, even if it's just to walk the dog. I'm never happy with what I'm wearing.

ORDER PROCESSOR, WATCH COMPANY, FEMALE, 25

Whenever I throw shoes out, I insist on keeping the shoelaces. I have hundreds that I'll probably never use. I expect that someday, if a lace breaks on one of my shoes, I'll have an extra one to replace it, but generally, the lace breaks when I'm away from home so it doesn't do much good.

SALESMAN, 55

When I button my shirt, I start with the neck and I button alternate buttons down until I reach the bottom. Then I come up skipping buttons upwards. The result is that I always leave one button open and I could never figure out why. I've been doing it this way for years.

MARKETING MANAGER, MALE, 43

I always check my fly before meeting people. You never know when things are going to be open at the wrong time.

JR: *Are you concerned that people may see you checking?*

Better that they see me checking than it being open!

GRAPHIC DESIGNER, MALE, 28

I'd rather go out and buy new underwear than do the laundry. There are about three drawers overflowing with underwear in my dresser.

MANUFACTURER, FEMALE, 33

It gives me a feeling of freedom and comfort to wear as little as possible. That's why I never wear underwear or socks. About three years ago, my wife bought me a dozen pair of underwear. All the packages have remained unopened except one and I only wore that pair once or twice. I do succumb once in awhile and wear socks for an important occasion. People look at me a little funny in the winter when they look down and don't see socks. It bothers them more than it bothers me.

CARPET SALESMAN, 30

I select clothing that I'm going to wear from the right side of my closet and put fresh clothes on the left. This system helps me decide what to wear.

SECRETARY, FEMALE, 44

66 The first article of clothing I put on in the morning is my hat. I always wear a wide-brimmed straw hat. If I have a shirt that has to go over my head, I don't remove the hat, I just pull it over the brim. **99**

SHUTTLE BUS DRIVER, MALE, 58

An old girlfriend of mine wears white socks when she has sex. Nothing else, just white socks. It serves a dual purpose. It seems she must wear something when she has sex, and also her toes get cold and the socks keep them warm.

GRADUATE STUDENT, MALE, 24
HIS EX-GIRLFRIEND IS A GRADUATE STUDENT, 23

When I'm playing poker and I win, I will take the same socks, shirt and underwear I won in with me and change into them for the next game and each game after that until I lose. This is normal for a poker player.

LADIES' APPAREL MANUFACTURER, MALE, 44

A friend of mine has a drawerful of new socks and puts on a brand-new pair every day. The kicker is that he throws them in the garbage after he wears them. I know this for a fact. I saw him do it. He doesn't like the feeling of socks that have already been worn or washed.

FABRIC SALESMAN, MALE, 24
HIS FRIEND IS AN APPAREL SALESMAN, 42

My husband has different color underwear for rainy and sunny days. He goes for light colors—whites, light blues and yellows—on sunny days and darker colors—navies and grays—on rainy or overcast days.

UNEMPLOYED, FEMALE, 28
HER HUSBAND IS A NECKWEAR MANUFACTURER, 28

I don't think I've ever thrown a shoe away in my life. I have a great collection of old shoes. My wife eventually throws some away when she can't stand it anymore but I just can't bring myself to do it. Shoes are more comfortable as they get older.

LAWYER, MALE, 55

I still can't give up the sixties look. I'll probably be an aging hippie forever.

SOCIAL WORKER, FEMALE, 56

There's a theory that no one loses a pair of socks—people lose one sock. Our maid does the laundry and I always got back one sock. I was losing socks right in my own house! It just occurred to me that if I pinned them together I'd get them back, so I started pinning my socks together before I put them in the hamper. Since I've been pinning them together I haven't lost any socks. And there are some additional benefits as well. The maid can now differentiate my socks from my wife's socks and my son's socks so she no longer mistakenly puts my socks in the wrong drawer. Also, now I don't have to fish around to match up two socks that are evenly worn down at the heel, particularly sweat socks.

EXECUTIVE MANAGING DIRECTOR, REAL ESTATE, MALE, 53

I wear my underpants over my panty hose to hold them up.

SECRETARY, FEMALE, 35

Before I put clean socks in the drawer, I roll them up into a little ball and then flip them. When I unflip them, one is always inside out and it's too much of a bother to change it early in the morning so I always wear one sock inside out.

SCHEDULING COORDINATOR, TELEVISION, MALE, 25

No one can ever put anything away in my closet. My clothes are arranged in a particular order and if it's disrupted, I can't function or get dressed. My shirts are filed according to sleeve length— sleeveless to short to long. The clothes are arranged from solids to plaids to stripes.

REAL ESTATE AGENT, FEMALE, 30

❝ My body is not a billboard so I won't wear anything with someone's logo on it. The only person I'll
advertise is myself. **❞**

STYLIST, MALE, 30

For about fifteen years now, I have not exactly repeated an outfit. I may wear the same suit but with a different shirt and tie. I have an extensive wardrobe and I get a big kick out of this.

LUGGAGE MANUFACTURER, MALE, 53

My boss has sixteen Lacoste sports shirts in different colors and he wears them in chromatic progression all through the summer. He starts with blue and goes right through the rainbow and then he starts all over again. He wears each one twice, but not two days in a row, before washing it and that way he manages to do the laundry only once for the entire summer. Sixteen shirts worn twice is good for six workday weeks. His entire summer wardrobe is planned in advance.

STUDENT, LIBRARY SCIENCE, FEMALE, 23
HER BOSS IS A LIBRARY SUPERVISOR, 33

I never untie the laces in my shoes. I use a shoehorn to get the shoes on because I'm too lazy to bother with the laces.

SUPERINTENDENT FOR GENERAL CONTRACTOR, MALE, 27

I have five different pairs of formal work shoes and I wear a different one each day of the work week, Monday through Friday, in order. If I don't go to work one day—Wednesday, let's say—I stay with the same sequence. I'll wear the third pair on Thursday.

MANAGEMENT CONSULTANT, MALE, 38

All the clothing in my closet is exceptionally organized. My suits are all together in one section, my pants are all together, my shirts are together and organized by color. If you go into my closet and you pick out the third tie, the third shirt, the third pair of pants and the third suit, that is a complete set. I drive my wife nuts.

SALES MANAGER, TELECOMMUNICATIONS, MALE, NEVER TELLS AGE

No matter where I go, I am never without my handbag. Whether I go to dinner or to the movies or just to get a cup of coffee, I have to have my handbag with me. I use the same one until it's worn out and then I change it. Occasionally I'll switch to a different one and feel out of sorts. Sometimes I try and break out and say to myself, "Okay, I'm just going around the corner for a coffee, I will only take my wallet," but I just feel so lost.

CFO, INTERNET COMPANY, FEMALE, 37

If you opened my closet you would see fifteen pairs of Khaki pants, and if you opened my dresser you would see twenty blue shirts. That's all that I've worn to work for as long as I can remember, although my neck size has gotten bigger over the years. They're all identical and they're all from L.L. Bean. Once I went to a meeting and my co-workers played a practical joke on me—they all came dressed in khaki pants and a blue shirt.

AUTOMOTIVE PARTS MANUFACTURER, MALE, 60

SCORE

Clothing is just a big cover-up, anyway.

If you've uncovered one to seven quirks: You are below average and probably have a whole closet full of polyester leisure suits.

Eight to sixteen: You're getting there. I suggest you try some of these on for size.

Over seventeen: You keep people in stitches. The best thing for you to wear is a disguise—so people don't recognize you.

66 When someone with a hat is walking down the street in front of me, I have this overwhelming urge to flip their hat off. Luckily, I've managed to keep this feeling under control, but I think it would be fun to follow through one of these days. **99**

ILLUSTRATOR, MALE, 23

66 When my team is in the lead, I will not change seats. If I go get a beer during a halftime break or period break, I will take the same seat when I come back. If my team is not playing well, only then will I switch seats. There have to be fifty million men in America that give you that one. 99

ATTORNEY, MALE, 39

Sportsmania

Woe is the sports enthusiast whose game lacks a signature good luck charm or ritualistic behavior. Hey, if you're not doing everything possible to win, you can't really call yourself a true sports fanatic.

Can sports quirks help you you eke out a victory...edge out an opponent...have the ball bounce your way? Who knows? Who cares? The simple fact is that personal idiosyncrasies make sports more exciting. Remember, it's not whether you win or lose, it's how you play the game. And the game is never played better than when it's played in a way that includes your quirkiest habits.

Good luck charms or peculiar behaviors add lots of excitement to your participation in sports—at little or no extra cost. And that's important because sports are an expensive luxury.

As a fan, you pay big bucks for the big tickets. And athletes: please bring your checkbook to the training facility because it takes a lot of gold to play for the Gold. But add a few idiosyncrasies and you add real value to your investment in sports.

Let's say it comes down to the last play of the game. Who gets more involved in these thrilling final seconds: the average sports fan, or the fanatic who's wearing a baseball cap upside down and inside out for good luck? The baseball-capped fan gets more out of the contest just by bringing something extra to the game.

The benefits of Sportsmania aren't limited to sports. They can be highly practical, too. Take the guy who keeps his ski rack on the car all year round. Peculiar? Maybe. Practical? Definitely, because the ski rack makes his car easy to spot in a parking lot.

You can really express your individuality and team spirit with just the right quirk. Read through the collection gathered here and then examine your own sports rituals to see whether you're a contender for Sportsmania.

A few years ago *Golf Digest* had an article on how to improve your balance. I really like playing golf and good balance is helpful in golf. Every morning since reading that article, I've followed the technique they recommended. They didn't say to do it in the shower—I came up with that on my own. I shampoo my hair and then put conditioner on my hair which I leave on for thirty seconds. I'll count 1,001, 1,002, up to 1,030, to make sure that it's on there for a full thirty seconds. For the first fifteen seconds I stand on my left leg with my right leg lifted up to work on my balance. For the last five seconds on my left leg I shut my eyes because shutting your eyes and standing on one leg is more difficult than having your eyes open. And for the next fifteen seconds I stand on my right leg with my left leg lifted up for ten seconds with my eyes open until the last five seconds when I shut my eyes and finish my counting.

JR: *You certainly make full use of your time—and your hair looks terrific!*

Thank you.

CEO, WIRELESS COMMUNICATIONS COMPANY, MALE, 50

Whenever I play soccer, as a goalkeeper, I wear two different colored socks for good luck.

JR: *Has it been lucky?*

Most of the time.

FIREMAN, 35

When I'm in a body-sculpting class or an aerobics class, I have to stand in the same spot each time or the whole class is out of sync.

JR: *What if it's not available?*

I'll squeeze very close to it. I come really early so that I can make sure that I get my spot.

FREELANCE CASTING DIRECTOR, FEMALE, 38

" The Green Bay Packers were playing the Denver Broncos in the Super Bowl a few years ago—I can't remember the score at this point but it was a very tight game. I told some people in the stands around me about a ritual that I have. In the final period or quarter of a sports event, if my team is losing, I will go to the bathroom and then something magical happens in favor of the team we're supporting. I had gone to the bathroom early in the fourth quarter and when I came back, they scored a touchdown, which put them ahead. Later, when it looked like we were going to be losing that lead in the final minutes of the game—this is after you've spent upwards of a grand or so on a seat—everyone in the stands was yelling at me, 'GO TO THE BATHROOM, GO TO THE BATHROOM!!' I did and the Broncos won the game! They were twelve-point underdogs. **"**

MANAGEMENT CONSULTANT, MALE, 38

If I have a bad round of golf on any particular day, I don't wear those shorts again for a very long time.

JR: *Does this technique seem to work?*

Well, in my demented mind, yes.

RETIRED SCHOOLTEACHER, FEMALE, 56

I play football and rugby and I will wear the practice shirt which I wore at the beginning of the season throughout the three or four months of the entire season without washing it. It gets brown and sticky from wearing it every day. Sometimes it will still be wet with sweat from the day before. In fact, rugby has two seasons a year and I once wore the same shirt for eight seasons without washing it once. Quirk, I guess.

JR: *Have you been doing well with it?*

I won two state championships.

SALESPERSON, FINANCIAL SERVICES, MALE, 22

Every morning when I get into work, I go on the Internet and look for every Mets article that I can find. I go to papers in New Jersey, and all the ones in New York, about fifteen altogether. I could be reading the same thing but I have to know what each one has to say. I even do this in the off-season. I'm interested in rumors or anything to do with the Mets.

INSURANCE SALESMAN, 34

When I turn on the television and I see that my sports team is losing, I believe that it's because I turned it on and I'm jinxing them, so I turn it off.

JR: *Does it seem to help your team?*

Absolutely not.

SALES MANAGER, INTERNET, MALE, 29

If I jog in Nike brand sneakers, then my everyday walking sneakers have to be Nike, even though I have other sneakers sitting around, such as Reebok and New Balance. I will not use them. I will only use the Nike sneakers—one brand at a time.

RESTAURATEUR, MALE, 58

If I am serving, my tennis partner insists that I use the same ball that we win a point with for my next serve. If we lose the point, she throws the ball across court and finds a completely different one so that I'm not jinxed.

STUDENT AND ACTRESS, FEMALE, 21

A friend and I are Buffalo Bills season ticket holders. We have a pregame ritual—we always get down on one knee and say a little prayer before the game, either in front of the television set or in the stadium. It worked about 90% of the time until they got to the Super Bowl. Unfortunately they lost four Super Bowls in a row.

PHARMACEUTICAL REPRESENTATIVE, MALE, 30

When we go to watch a Grimsby (that's our hometown in England) town soccer game, our friend wears his Grimsby town shirt. Before the game we all rub the emblem on the shirt for good luck. Out of the fifteen games we've gone to see in the last couple of years, we've only lost about two times.

RESEARCHER, RECRUITMENT COMPANY, MALE, 26
HIS FRIEND IS A BAR MANAGER, 29

I wear a baseball cap playing most sports and when I'm doing poorly, I turn the cap around front to back or back to front with the hope of changing the momentum and improving the situation. It's called *Rally Caps*.

PROGRAMMER, MALE, 23

When I buy a new pair of jogging sneakers, I take a pen and label them with the letter "R" for running and the date I purchased them on the outer side of each sneaker. I keep track of how many miles I've run in my datebook. After a number of miles or a number of months, I'll have used up all the structure and springiness in the sneaker. At that stage, I write the letter "W" under the "R" signifying that they have now become walking sneakers and can no longer be used for running.

JR: *You wouldn't know that without labeling them?*

That's correct—I have about six pairs of sneakers. I label both the left and right sneaker because if I buy two pairs of the same brand, I wouldn't know which one is the R and which one is the W.

JR: *Which brand seems to last longer?*

New Balance is pretty good.

MANAGEMENT CONSULTANT, MALE, 55

I wash my golf balls in the dishwasher once or twice a week so they're nice and shiny when I play.

RETIRED SCHOOLTEACHER, FEMALE, 56

When I go fishing I always spit on my worm for good luck. My friend here used to catch all the fish so I spit on my worm once and I caught fish before he did so I kept on doing it.

JR: *Has it continued to be successful for you?*

Yes, it has, otherwise I wouldn't be doing it.

DIRECTOR OF TRANSPORTATION, COLLEGE, MALE, 62

Every night, before I go to sleep, I have to know whether the Red Sox won. In fact, I won't go to sleep until I go online and find out the final scores.

GRADUATE STUDENT, MALE, 26

I keep skis on the roof of my car all year round so I can find my car in a parking lot. Other people may leave the rack on the roof in the winter but no one actually keeps the skis there because they're afraid of being ripped off. Mine are old and in very bad condition so no one's ever taken them. The big disadvantages to this are that my car is well known to my friends and I can't go to an automatic car wash so my car is always dirty.

PHYSICIAN, MALE, 28

You should mark your golf balls in a way that is specifically identifiable to you. What I do is draw a straight line on my golf balls in red or green depending on how I feel that day. Green if I'm going to go for it and red if I'm going to play more conservatively. No one can claim it as their own—it can only be mine. In addition to helping me to identify my golf ball, it helps me to line it up better when I'm trying to make a putt since it's a straight line. I've been doing this for many years.

JR: *Has anyone followed your example and marked theirs in some unique way?*

No, as far as I know, I'm the only person with this technique in the history of golf!

CEO, WIRELESS COMMUNICATIONS COMPANY, MALE, 50

Four is my lucky number and I play well with it. I got a shirt once with a four on it and I requested a four again from my coach.

STUDENT, FEMALE, 12

My brother-in-law, David, puts a glass figurine of a dolphin on the television set for good luck for his team, the Miami Dolphins, when they play. He believes that it will help them win. It's weird, I know.

OWNER, ADVERTISING AGENCY, MALE, 40
HIS BROTHER-IN-LAW IS A FINANCIAL PLANNER, 31

❝ I love fishing but I hate to bait my own hook or pull the fish off the hook. It smells up my fingers so I have my friend do it for me. If my friend isn't available, I don't go fishing. **❞**

CLOTHING SALESMAN, 29

When I play golf I only use coins minted in the 1960s to mark my golf balls so that I will shoot in the 60s. It can be any coin but it must be minted in the '60s. If I'm playing poorly, I think that perhaps the coin that I'm using which is minted in the '60s had been spending a lot of time touching a coin minted in the '70s or '80s and then I have to throw that coin away and get a new coin. That's the excuse I reach for.

GOLF JOURNALIST, MALE, 37

I find it practical to wash baseball caps in the dishwasher. I put them on the top rack so the logos don't melt in the hot water. Dishwashing detergent removes the enzymes, like perspiration, in bodily fluid. Liquid dishwashing detergent is more effective than granular detergent because it washes out a little bit better. And, best of all, the baseball caps don't get squished in the dishwasher like they do in the clothes washer.

DIRECTOR OF CONSTRUCTION, FEMALE, 55

I like to keep shoe trees in my sneakers because it gives them a much better look. The peculiar part is that I don't keep them in my other shoes.

PRINTING INK MANUFACTURER, MALE, LATE 40s

If I watch the first game of a playoff series at a bar and my team wins while I am at that bar, I have to go back and continue to watch the rest of the series at that same bar. But if they come off the first game losing, then I can't go back to that bar until the series is over. This is a strategy I strictly adhere to for all sports. I just used it for the Yankees for baseball. And when they're in the playoffs, I do it for the Knicks for basketball, for the Rangers for hockey and for the Jets for football.

ELECTRICIAN, MALE, 32

Since you're not using my name I can confide this. I wear regular panties under my tennis skirt, not tennis panties. I bought a navy blue pair of panties to match my navy blue tennis skirt and red panties to match my red tennis skirt and they were much less expensive than tennis panties. I never use pockets for balls anyway because I don't want to get my clothes dirty. I can't imagine that anyone would notice or care, except possibly my husband because he's a play-by-the-rules type of guy so I haven't told him. So far when a breeze blew my skirt up a little, the tennis police haven't come onto the court and arrested me.

E-COMMERCE CONSULTANT, FEMALE, 31

I root for whichever team the guy I'm dating is rooting for.

DESKTOP PUBLISHER, FEMALE, 23

I played soccer in high school and college, and I wore Adidas socks that had the logo on only one side and it was meant to be worn on the outside of your calf. I would wear two left socks as a good luck thing.

JR: *Did you throw out the right socks?*

No, I'd use those for practice.

BUSINESS CONSULTANT, MALE, 22

My college roommate kept his cleats outside so, of course, they were cold. He would bring them in and warm them up in the microwave before playing football on Sunday mornings. One time he actually burned a hole inside his cleats and left the entire house smelling of burned rubber. The microwave wasn't ruined but the house stunk of rubber for about three or four days. He had to get new cleats.

ASSISTANT MEDIA PLANNER, ADVERTISING, MALE, 26
HIS FRIEND IS AN ENGINEER, 25

I played baseball for four years in college and one year in minor league baseball. Before entering the batter's box I'd have to flip the bat over and draw my significant other's initials in the sand with the bat. Next to the initial would be my number, 22. It was done in a matter of seconds. You wouldn't even notice it. Then I'd step in and I would bless myself, crucifix gesture. And, like a lot of baseball players, I would never step on a white line out in the field. Also, when running out to shortstop, at third base I would have to touch third first and run out for the position. There's more. When the pitcher delivered the ball, I'd have to wet the fingers of my throwing hand and smack my glove twice. After that I'd hitch my right foot back and forth to get my balance going. In baseball you always want to be moving when the pitch is delivered. It's kind of like a tempo, a stutterstep thing.

Consistency, ask any ballplayer. You get in a routine. Look at Turk Wendell, relief pitcher, middle reliever for the Mets—he was very superstitious. When he was out on the field, he brushed his teeth between every inning. Wade Boggs ate fried chicken before every single game of his career. He was about 38 years old when he retired so he probably played seventeen or eighteen seasons and he frequently played 162 games a year. Think about it …that's 162 baseball games in a year, and he ate fried chicken before every single game!

EXECUTIVE RECRUITER, MALE, 30

We have a Pitt [University of Pittsburgh] flag that we bought on a Friday many years ago. It says Pitt and it has the panther on it. When the Pittsburgh Steelers play, my son and my husband must fly the flag on the flagpole outside our house and it must be outside starting on Friday. If they don't put it out Friday, they don't fly it because they feel that they will put the jinx on the team and they won't win.

OFFICE MANAGER, FEMALE, 52

❝ My friend wears all her gold jewelry all the time because she's been ripped off three times in her apartment. She sleeps and does gymnastics wearing it. She has these massive rings on all her fingers; gobs of bracelets, at least twelve on each arm; and chains dripping down her front. I don't know how she manages to hold her body up. She never, ever takes them off. **❞**

UNEMPLOYED, FEMALE, 41
HER FRIEND IS A STEWARDESS, 41

One time I scored three goals in soccer and when I looked back and analyzed what I did differently, I noticed that I had accidentally put my underwear on inside out. Ever since then I have a habit of wearing my underwear inside out for good luck during the game. Eventually, my luck with the underwear technique ran out so I decided to try putting a penny in my right sneaker. Now in addition to wearing my underwear inside out, I also put a penny in my right sneaker for good luck. And to ensure that I am doing everything possible on my behalf to win, I also step into the soccer field with my right foot before the game.

STUDENT AND LIFEGUARD, MALE, 24

For soccer, I wear only red underwear. They're lucky for me.

MERCHANDISE ANALYST, MALE, 22

My golf partner keeps a string in his pocket which he uses to measure the distance between his feet so they are the exact same distance apart each time he positions himself to drive a golf ball.

JR: *Is he a good golfer?*

No, but he'd probably be even worse if he didn't use the string.

LAWYER, MALE, 55
HIS FRIEND IS A LAWYER, 50s

SCORE

If you recognize six or fewer quirkularities: Take a breather on the bench. You need to take some time to reconsider your game.

Seven to twelve of these ring true: That's the spirit! You want to win, but not go overboard with so many quirks that you end up facing the team from Bellevue!

Scored thirteen to twenty-six: Hello?! Sports. Life. Make a choice!

66 When I enter an elevator, I take a deep breath and hold it during the entire ride. I pray that I don't meet anyone I know so I won't be forced to exhale and start a conversation and inhale everyone's germs. 99

JEWELRY MANUFACTURER, MALE, 35

The Howard Hughes Syndrome

We have *not* seen the enemy but we know they're out there… waiting…armed and dangerous…ready to attack us at any time. They're the dreaded G-E-R-M-S! There's no escaping these microscopic, pesky viruses and bacteria which lurk *everywhere* and multiply *endlessly*. We Goliaths must utilize every means possible to outwit these fearsome Davids. Germs are most potent, most prevalent and most difficult to combat in and around:

MOUTHS

To protect yourself from possible contamination if someone

should ask for a sip of your drink, here's what I recommend:

A. Carefully observe exact location where his/her mouth has made contact and avoid that spot.

B. Offer to save some for him/her.

C. Say, "Why don't you finish it, I'm really not thirsty." Option C has extra bonus of being thought of as nice guy.

D. Smile when drink is returned and pour into nearest plant when he/she is not looking.

E. Offer to buy one for him/her. Option E is least desirable because of the expense.

Exception 1: When we kiss people. When we kiss people, the germs move over.

Exception 2: Eating from other people's plates. Other people's plates are relatively germ-free. Especially if it has Häagen-Dazs coffee ice cream on it.

TOOTHBRUSHES

No matter how much you wash or shake another person's toothbrush, the germs do not fall off. They cling. So you must never use another person's toothbrush. Not even the toothbrush of someone you kiss. If you keep your toothbrush in the same holder as another person, however, the germs cannot jump onto your toothbrush. Even if their toothbrush is in the adjacent hole. But only if the bristles do not touch.

DERRIERES

Derrieres are full of very bad germs. So you must never sit directly on someone else's toilet. You can cover the germs with paper and hope that they do not crawl above it. Or you can squat and hope that they do not like what they see a whole lot.

MONEY

These are the least harmful germs. We can easily coexist with them.

The few areas from which germs are repelled:

• *Bloomingdale's*. Everything in Bloomingdale's is guaranteed germ-free. In fact, they are highly recommended for your health.

• *Mel Gibson*.

• *Certain foods*. You can apply the following principle to determine which foods do not have a lot of germs: The greater the calories, the fewer the germs. A flaming chocolate crêpe has virtually no germs.

And with that, I wash my hands of this.

66 Every time I touch money, no matter how often, I wash my hands. When I hand my husband money for tolls while he's driving, I wipe my hands on a wet rag which I always keep in the car for that purpose. If I find money on the sidewalk, I use a tissue to pick it up and wrap it with, and when I get home, I wash the coin or bill with soap and water. 99

ASSISTANT UPHOLSTERER, FEMALE, 59

I press the buttons on the elevator (inside or outside the elevator) with my knuckle. I saw a program where they took samples from objects that are commonly touched by many people—ATM buttons, elevator buttons, and so forth—and they did a bacteriological analysis of them. They're horrible and disgusting.

VICE PRESIDENT, WOMEN'S APPAREL MANUFACTURER, MALE, 40

I can't remember the last time I used a public bathroom, it was that long ago. I don't believe doctors who say you can't contract a social disease by sitting on a dirty toilet.

SALESMAN, 26

I bring a sheet with me when I travel just in case the sheet in the hotel isn't clean enough. I'll put mine over theirs so I don't have to lie on a sheet that I think is dirty. Then I pull the blanket all the way down so it doesn't touch me.

JR: *Has the housekeeper ever taken your sheet by mistake?*

No, I take it off in the morning because it's humiliating.

EXECUTIVE, SURVEY RESEARCH, FEMALE, 49

I try never to touch food even if my hands are clean. If there is a napkin available, I'll wrap it around the sandwich or whatever it is I'm eating. If not, I'll eat all around the spot I'm holding and throw that piece away.

ARCHITECT, MALE, 37

I insist that my secretary clean the receiver of my telephone with disinfectant every morning. I must start the day with an immaculately clean phone.

PROFESSIONAL INVESTOR, MALE, 37

I always hold a coffee cup that has a handle in my left hand even though I'm right-handed. My reasoning is that there are fewer left-handed people in the world so fewer people drink on that side of the cup. Therefore, in my mind, there are less germs there.

GRAPHIC DESIGNER, FEMALE, 30

I drink where the handle of the cup is because no one drinks there.

MUSICIAN, FEMALE, 28

When I get into a taxi, I never let any bare part of my body touch the seat. I sit forward so the back of my head doesn't touch the back of the seat. And I wear gloves all year so my hands don't contact anything directly that masses of people have used.

SALESWOMAN, 29

There's no way I'll go into a swimming pool because people urinate in the water and go in with different skin diseases and God knows what else. I will go into the ocean because it's so vast and because the wastes don't seem to bother the fish.

TAILOR, MALE, 47

When my husband and I go to the movies, I take a washable coat with me to change into before I enter the theater because most movie theaters are dirty and I don't want to contaminate my good coat or clothing and then have to hang it in my closet.

FEMALE, 80

No matter how heavy a shopping bag is that I'm carrying, I will never put it down on the floor. It would get disgusting germs all over it.

HOUSEWIFE, 59

When my father goes on vacation he takes his own silverware and salt and pepper with him. My mother is embarrassed, she thinks he's a nut.

TEACHER, FEMALE, 25
HER FATHER IS RETIRED, 73

I have a habit of rinsing any kitchenware such as glasses, china and silverware before using it even if it just came out of the dishwasher. When I'm in someone else's home and I serve myself, I rinse everything but try not to make it too obvious. Of course, I can't do it if I'm being served. In a restaurant I will wipe everything with a wet napkin. It's the strangest thing.

BUSINESS STRATEGY CONSULTANT, MALE, 30

I find it extremely unsanitary and unacceptable when the person behind the counter grabs an ice-cream cone that doesn't have a paper liner on it with his bare hand before putting the scoop of ice cream in it. Frequently, he gives you a napkin when he hands you the ice cream. Why doesn't he use the napkin to pick up the cone in the first place? It drives me up a wall—I don't want anyone to touch my ice-cream cone. *Ugh!*

SPEECH PATHOLOGIST, FEMALE, 26

I like the toilet paper facing toward the back because less dust settles on it.

ANALYST, BANK, FEMALE, MID-30s

I try to balance myself in the subway as best as possible so I don't have to touch the pole. If it's a bumpy ride then I pull the sleeve of my shirt down and touch the pole with the sleeve so I don't have to make direct contact. It grosses me out.

HAIR COLORIST, MALE, 27

My quirk is that I will not let anybody drink from my glass or eat from my plate. *Nobody. Ever.* Not even my family, my boyfriend or my friends. Someone just asked me for a sip and I told them that when I was finished, I'd leave something over.

NURSE, FEMALE, 33

I feel more comfortable tearing off and discarding the first few squares of toilet paper in a public bathroom because it may have been contaminated by the previous person using that stall.

BUSINESS DEVELOPMENT, NEW MEDIA, FEMALE, 33

I always break Q-tips before I use them. Somehow, I always think that germs would travel from one end to the other so by breaking them, they can't get across.

LAWYER, MALE, 31

An out-of-town friend of mine came to visit for a few weeks and I noticed when I went into the bathroom that his toothbrush was sticking up in the holder. So I pushed it down. The next time I went into the bathroom, it was pushed back up so I pushed it down again. This went on for a while until I finally asked him about it. He explained that the idea of the bristles actually touching the holder which is full of bacteria really turned him off. That's why he twists his toothbrush so it doesn't slide all the way down.

ACCOUNT EXECUTIVE, FEMALE, 29
HER FRIEND IS A DRAFTSMAN, 31

I put sponges in the dishwasher because it sterilizes them. My wife doesn't like the dirt from the sponge mixing with the plates and silverware so I started microwaving the sponges. You wet them and microwave them and then it just boils.

PSYCHOLOGIST, MALE, 46
HIS WIFE IS A HOMEMAKER, 48

66 My mother sprays my father all over his body with Lestoil before he gets into bed. He doesn't take a shower every day and she thinks he may have germs. She disinfects the poor man. **99**

WAITRESS, 40
HER MOTHER IS A HOUSEWIFE, 59

When I go through a revolving door, I put my hand on the highest possible spot that I can reach to push it hoping that there are fewer germs there since fewer people have touched it.

SALES DIRECTOR, JEWELRY COMPANY, MALE, 34

When making a salad or preparing a drink, if a piece of lettuce or an ice cube falls into the sink, it's immediately thrown away, regardless of how clean the sink may be. It's my crazy thing about germs. If someone else is making a drink and I know the ice cube fell into the sink but was used anyway, I will politely drink it but it will bother me tremendously.

COLLEGE PROFESSOR, MALE, 38

I towel-dry my hair and if the towel falls on the floor, I have to use a new towel for fear that germs and bacteria are on the floor.

COMPUTER PROGRAMMER, MALE, 29

This lunatic I knew in law school was obsessed with germs. When he went to a public toilet, he would not touch any surface directly without using paper. He would take a paper towel to open and close the stall, do his business, flush with his foot, then tear off pieces of toilet paper to open the stall door and to turn on the faucet. Then he'd get another piece of paper to open the door. So you'd always see him walking out of the bathroom with a piece of paper in his hand.

LAWYER, MALE, 41
HIS FRIEND IS A LAWYER, 32

Before I open a can, I wash the top off with soap and water so any dirt or germs don't get inside as I'm opening it. That's what my mother told me.

BANKER, MALE, 26

I always felt that if I touched the area between my toes, I would get germs on my hands. To avoid contacting there directly, I use a cloth or a Q-tip or just spread my toes, drip the soap in and let the water run over my feet.

DIAMOND DEALER, MALE, 55

In a cafeteria, such as the one at work, there are usually two kinds of trays, cups and plates. Reusable ones that are rewashed for those people who are staying to eat and disposable cardboard, paper or styrofoam ones for people who are leaving with their food. Regardless of whether I'm staying or going, I take the disposable ones because I'm turned off by the reusable ones which never seem clean enough. I confuse my lunch companions because they know that we decided to stay yet they see me with all the "to go" items. I have to lie to the people behind the counter who want to know whether I'm going or staying. I say I'm going when actually I'm staying with all my disposable accessories.

ACCOUNT EXECUTIVE, MARKETING, 28

SCORE

Use this table to determine whether you are suffering from a mild or severe case of *The Howard Hughes Syndrome*:

Less than five similar: You're the type who would ask for a sip of my Coke.

Five to ten: You're the type who would ask for a sip of my Coke but would wipe the bottle rim first.

Over ten: You would rather die than ask for a sip of my Coke. In fact, you would order tea because it's been boiled. But you would request a paper cup and wipe the spoon.

" Rather than lug the vacuum cleaner around, chasing after the dirt, I bring the dirt to the vacuum cleaner. I keep the vacuum cleaner inside a closet and just sweep the dirt there. All I have to do is reach in, push the button and suction up the dirt. **"**

PAPER SALESMAN, 50

Now I've Heard Everything!

Ever notice how you stop and give a perfectly smooth, flat side-walk your nastiest, most accusing how-dare-you look after you've tripped over your own two feet?

Do you wait for the phone to ring at least twice before answering even if it's right beside you?

How many times do you check the knobs on your stove to make sure they're off before you leave the house?

Are you twirling your hair? Ah, hah! I caught you in action.

Do you refuse to buy the top newspaper on a stack even though it's in perfect condition? *Now tell me that's not a quirk!*

And when you're at a newsstand and you flip through a magazine and you decide to buy that magazine, do you reach for another copy because the one you were flipping through is no longer new?

Did you start reading the last page of this book first?

Are you twirling your hair again?

Sound familiar? Are you considering making an extra appointment with your therapist? *Forget it.* If you do most or even all of these things, you've got plenty of company. These are some of the more common unconscious little rituals and habits we all share.

Some idiosyncrasies you might be somewhat embarrassed about, others you claim sole ownership to because of their ingeniousness. People will either think of you fondly because of them or it will irk the hell out of them and they won't want anything to do with you. Let's face it, they're what make you, you.

The trick to appearing normal is to hang out with people who are crazier than you.

But the bottom line is...*nobody's playing with a full deck.*

My ex-boss has a device above his desk that looks somewhat like a clock. It has the numbers one through ten and the words *Bell Ringer* on it in a circle and a movable cardboard hand. He uses it as a rating system for the work that is presented to him. It used to drive us crazy. He'd sit there for half an hour and not say a word about the work after the person did three hours of singing and dancing and carrying on and then he would get up and move the dial to one of the numbers or all the way up to *Bell Ringer*, depending on how little or how much he liked the idea.

COPYWRITER, FEMALE, 36
HER EX-BOSS IS A VICE PRESIDENT, AD AGENCY, 50

When I go home to my apartment, although I know there's nobody there because I live alone, I always yell, "Hello, I'm home!"

SOUND ENGINEER, MALE, 31

From the time I was about three, there was an old cliché that if you stepped on a crack, you'd break your mother's back. So, to this day, at the age of fifty, I still tend to avoid the cracks in the sidewalk as I'm walking along.

PHYSICIAN, MALE, 50

When I read, see or think about something, I will mentally type out the thought on my toes. My little toes control the shift keys and I use my big toes for the space bar. I'm real fast at it too.

MODEL, FEMALE, 24

When I look at consecutive letters on a license plate, I try to form a word out of it. For example, if I see GLS on a license plate, that would spell glass. Or QRK would spell quirk. It's satisfying if I can form a word out of the letters.

ASSISTANT TO TALENT AGENT, MALE, 25

Normal couples have arguments over the toothpaste tube, we have constant hassles about the car armrest. She likes it up for her pocketbook, I like it down for my arm. When I do the driving, I insist on having it down and move her pocketbook over to her side.

PHYSICIAN, MALE, 28

I read the newspaper from the back page to the front. I think it's because the better stuff is on the front page and I like to gradually build up to it.

PRIVATE INVESTOR, MALE, 61

My cleaning lady comes on Mondays. I'm never quite sure whether she's coming in the morning or the afternoon because she's not on a specific schedule, but by nine or ten o'clock Sunday evening, I start to get anxious because I know that I have to clean up for the cleaning lady. I force my husband to straighten up and I make piles so she can at least vacuum around them. The house needs to be clean enough for the cleaning lady to come.

COMMERCIAL REAL ESTATE BROKER, FEMALE, 31

As soon as I sit down at my desk, I open the top middle desk drawer. I leave it open the entire time I sit there. For some reason I feel terribly uncomfortable if it's closed.

SECURITY GUARD, FEMALE, 19

Our mother didn't want us using language that was offensive so she would make up words for private body parts or nasty things. I was convinced until I got to school that vagina was called *tooshy*. She felt that *tooshy* sounded more pleasant. When I got to school, my friends enlightened me as to what it's really called.

MANAGER, AEROSPACE ENGINEERING, FEMALE, 39
HER MOTHER IS A RETIRED SECRETARY, 62

One of the small satisfactions in my life is drawing a red line through an item on a list of things I'm supposed to do. It's one thing finished in a frustrating, unfinished world. I'll even add something I've accomplished to the list which was not originally on it. Then I have the gratification of crossing it off.

HOMICIDE DETECTIVE, FEMALE, 46

I cannot sit in a restaurant or any public place with my back to the major entrance. I like to see who's coming in.

WRITER, MALE, 29

One Sunday when I was in the army, all my friends were away on a weekend pass and I was stuck with guard duty. I was walking up and down a lonely road with my rifle singing *My Melancholy Baby*. Ever since then, when I go buy my newspaper every Sunday, I quietly sing *My Melancholy Baby* on the way there.

CARPENTER, MALE, 59

I love to watch Spanish television and movies for hours at a time and I don't understand a word of Spanish. It keeps me entertained.

LADIES' SPORTSWEAR MANUFACTURER, MALE, 30

I save shopping bags from stores and organize them alphabetically. I have a couple of dozen, mostly from department stores such as Barneys, Lord & Taylor, Macy's, Neiman Marcus, Nordstrom and Saks Fifth Avenue. I use them to transport things occasionally.

FULL-TIME MOM, 43

I never tell my age. My ex-wife or her lawyer don't even know my age.

BUSINESS EXECUTIVE, MALE

❝ My father thinks it's New Year's every Fourth of July. We have a big Fourth of July party every year and he keeps checking his watch. When it's twelve o'clock, he says, 'Happy New Year!' **❞**

WAITRESS, 40
HER FATHER IS A CABDRIVER, 67

I can't ride backwards in any moving vehicle. I'm a commuter and I have to be facing in the direction that the bus or train is traveling because I think that the ride will be faster.

INTERNET STRATEGIST, MALE, 28

My friend reads the last page of a book first just in case he dies—he'll know what happened at the end.

COLLEGE STUDENT, MALE, 18
HIS FRIEND IS A COLLEGE STUDENT, 18

I have to break a date with a guy three times before I finally agree to go out with him. I like the persistent ones.

JR: *Do most call back?*

A lot of them don't. Just the ones that find me worth waiting for.

JEWELRY MANUFACTURER, FEMALE, 33

My aunt will wash, curl and dry her hair at home before going to the hairdresser. She likes to look her best at all times, including on her way to get her hair done.

HOUSEWIFE, 29
HER AUNT IS A SEAMSTRESS, 49

When entering almost any indoor place I empty my pockets and put the contents in one little pile. It generally contains my eye-glasses, pen, key, wristwatch and money. In a restaurant, for example, my little spot is one corner of the table. I believe it's a way of expressing my territoriality. It becomes my little spot and if anybody else puts something on my little spot, it bothers me, and I will move my things or theirs. I've never lost anything because all I have to do is remove it all and put everything back in my pocket when I'm ready to leave.

COLLEGE PROFESSOR, MALE, 38

Every Sunday I do the puzzle in the magazine section of The New York Times. I never have time to read the paper so I do the puzzle and throw the paper out. One day I was doing my puzzle in a hotel in Massachusetts and a stranger walked over to me and said, "Do you find that you do the puzzle and throw the paper away?" And it's true—I don't think I realized it until he said that to me!

OWNER, TEXTILE BUSINESS, FEMALE, 70

When I'm tired or upset or depressed, I get a towel, fold it, put it in my mouth, and scream like a maniac. Then I feel better!

HAIRDRESSER, MALE, 25

At the age of thirty, I still read comic books. I have a subscription to ten of them…Batman, Superman, Aquaman—all of them. During the week, the pressures of the job are too much so who wants to read about global warming or the state of the economy. I'd rather read about Batman catching criminals.

LADIES' SPORTSWEAR MANUFACTURER, MALE, 30

My husband would rather drive miles out of his way than ask for directions. He says he's not willing to take somebody else's directions, he likes to be in control. He's right. He has excellent control over how to waste time and gasoline and where to find the most uninteresting places. I've been on the road more than a traveling salesman. Whenever I sit down, I expect trees to pass by.

HOUSEWIFE, 45
HER HUSBAND IS AN EXECUTIVE, 52

When I pick up my mail, if it looks like one piece is interesting, say, a love note, or a check from somebody who's past due, I save that letter for last. When I have time to savor it, then I open it.

TEXTILE WHOLESALER, MALE, 33

My neighbors think I'm crazy. I don't cut the lawn in the normal, up-and-down way. I cut it in spiral fashion, working from the outside around toward the center. I love the way the tracks look when it's cut.

CHAUFFEUR, MALE, 25

On any screw-on cap, I'll screw it on three times and that's the end of it. If it isn't completely screwed on, it doesn't matter.

NURSE, FEMALE, 28

If I'm given a sheet of ruled paper to write on, I automatically write either perpendicular or diagonal to the rules because I don't need somebody else to organize me. I can organize myself.

SAILOR, MALE, 43

When I go to a movie with my date, I buy two tickets but I manage to hand them only one as we're walking in, so I have an extra one. When we come out, I look for someone interesting waiting in line to buy a ticket and I hand them my extra one. I just say, "Here, enjoy the movie." People are interesting. When I give them the ticket, they never say anything, they're so stunned. They just look at the ticket in amazement as I walk away. I've done it over a hundred times during the last ten years and it works about 75% to 80% of the time. When I'm caught, I always have the extra ticket. It's my way of feeling a little like Robin Hood—stealing from the rich and giving to the poor.

SALESMAN, 29

Before I take something from someone—food, paper, wrappers, pencil, anything—I smell it first. I put my head forward and sniff before I touch.

STOCKBROKER, FEMALE, 34

I never smile. I don't want to put any wrinkles in my face.

JR: *What if you hear a good joke?*

I never smile.

JR: *Do you have all your teeth?*

Yes.

TAXI DRIVER, MALE, 37
(THIS WAS CONFIRMED BY HIS FRIENDS AND NOTHING I COULD SAY
WOULD MAKE HIM SMILE!)

To be able to read anything, even a personal letter, I must hold a
pen or a pencil in my hand although I don't use it. It probably
stems from my school days when I used to underline in the text-
books and now I find the habit has stayed with me.

ASSISTANT BANK TREASURER, FEMALE, WOULD NOT GIVE AGE

I have to be completely naked when I'm cleaning.

THEATER DIRECTOR, FEMALE, 29

I find myself counting the steps from one place to another, such as
from the bus stop to my home or from my garage to my home.
From the bus stop to my home there are 240 steps, walking at a
leisurely pace. From my garage to my home, there are 360 steps.
Why I do this, I don't know. It has no practical value although I
can't see any harm in doing it!

PHYSICIAN, MALE, 64

I like the resonant sound when I pat my stomach. I play it to the
rhythm of music that's playing or some tune that's going through
my head. I'll deny this if you ever mention it to my patients.

PHYSICIAN, MALE, 36
(HE DID A GREAT DEMONSTRATION!)

❝I enjoy smoking cigarettes stuck between the prongs of a fork or at the end of a straw.

JR: Does it work at the end of a straw?

It works very well at the end of a straw.

JR: Why do you do this?

To break up the monotony of the day. I'm not even conscious of when I do it.**❞**

ADMINISTRATIVE ASSISTANT, MALE, 25

I save every single plastic bag—I can't bring myself to throw them away. I have to recycle them and if I have no immediate use for them, I let them build up. I probably have at least 300 to 400 bags at home. My wife goes crazy. She's always telling me to get rid of them but I just can't throw away a perfectly good bag.

ACCOUNTANT, MALE, 34

I have to get rid of all plastic bags, paper shopping bags, containers and lids from take-out restaurants, yogurt containers—any bag or container. And my wife likes to save all of them. It's annoying when you open the closet door and they all fall out. Personally, I think they're unnecessary—they accumulate and you don't use them anyway. If I see a plastic bag on the counter which I know someone has set aside to save, I throw it out. It's upsetting to my wife and my in-laws. When my in-laws come for the weekend, they always bring some goodies for my boys. My mother-in-law will carefully fold the bags thinking that when she leaves on Sunday, she'll have bags to carry some empty containers or other items back in but she knows that if I get my hands on it—straight into the garbage. It's an ongoing argument.

APPAREL SALESMAN, 48

When I'm walking down the street with a date, I'll have my date walk near the curb and I will walk close to the buildings in case a car skids. It will hit him first.

PHYSICAL EDUCATION TEACHER, FEMALE, 23

My reverse quirk is that I make an effort to break any habit or any consistent thing that I might be doing. If I find I've done something a certain way six times in a row and it can be done another way, I will deliberately do it another way.

CPA, MALE, 46

When I visit someone and there's more than one entrance to their home, I must leave through the same door I came in. Under no circumstances will I leave through a different doorway. If I go in the front door, I go out the front door. If I go in the back, I go out the back.

MANAGER OF CONSUMER AFFAIRS, CORPORATION, FEMALE, 37

I'm a neat freak. When a perforated form has been torn off, I'll tear off every little piece that's been left on. Also, if something is stapled in a manner that is not nice and neat, I will take the staple out, adjust the papers so they're positioned exactly in line, and then re-staple it.

OFFICE MANAGER, TELEVISION NETWORK, FEMALE, 39

I've been saving all my fingernails and toenails in an old mayonnaise jar since I was in the ninth grade. I put a little Brut in there so it smells good, although protein doesn't decay. I just got into the habit and it's hard to break.

His attractive wife: It's true. Sometimes, as a joke, he shows it to our visitors.

SALES MANAGER, JEWELRY COMPANY, MALE, 29

There is no way I can start working until I sharpen all my pencils and line them up. It just feels neat and orderly and kind of organizes my thoughts.

LAWYER, MALE, 31

I count things. I count the squares in a chain-link fence. I count the windows in a building, the tiles in a wall—anything with definite divisions running in a pattern. I haven't the foggiest idea why.

ATTORNEY, MALE, 35

If I'm in my car and I realize I've forgotten something, I won't back up, even if there isn't any traffic and I'm only a few feet from my house. I have to go all the way around the block to come back. I feel as though I'm not progressing if I go over the same path.

PRESSER, DRY CLEANING STORE, MALE, 30

I like to perform for the cameras that surround me in my life. From time to time I put on a show in elevators or at ATM machines where a camera is always watching. I'll wave hello or make stupid faces or pretend I'm Bruce Lee. I did some karate kicks a little while ago in the elevator of my apartment building. The doorman must have seen me on the monitor because as I was walking out the door, he said, "Oh, you're dangerous!"

RECRUITER, MALE, 25

If there's a specific article in the fourth section of the newspaper that I want to read, I can't just open the paper to that article. I must start with page one and read from the beginning, in order, up to that column.

ACTOR, 42

I love to move my apartment furniture around. I like change for the sake of change. Not only does the placement of the furniture change, the use of the room changes as well. The living room can become the bedroom, the bedroom can become another room, my son's room can become my room. Sometimes I like sleeping in a large room and sometimes I like sleeping in a small room. I had a couch in the kitchen for a while, which was great. When my son comes home from a holiday, he never knows where his room will be or which room is being used for what because it's always different. It's become a family joke.

DANCER, FEMALE, 38

I like to walk around the apartment naked and I love young men. That's why I'm with one.

FEMALE, 63

When my mother includes some good news or a happy thought in a letter, she'll put a little smiling face after the sentence. If she has a bit of bad news or a sad comment, for example, "the old dog died," she'll put a little frowning face after the sentence.

SEA CAPTAIN, MALE, 41
HIS MOTHER IS A HOUSEWIFE, 61

My girlfriend puts on her makeup—mascara and all—the night before to save time in the morning.

SECRETARY, FEMALE, 22
HER GIRLFRIEND IS A STUDENT, 22

When I want to remember something in the morning, I take a paper napkin, poke a hole through it and hang it on the doorknob. When I leave my apartment, the napkin reminds me that there was something I wanted to remember, like taking oranges with me to the office or stopping at the shoemaker to have my boots fixed and so on. There was only one time that I couldn't remember what it was that I had to do.

BOOKKEEPER, FEMALE, 46

I fake a sneeze when I fart so people won't hear me.

STUDENT, FEMALE, 17

Before I discard an empty container, whether it's an empty tube of toothpaste or a jar, I always put the cap back on it.

INVESTMENT ANALYST, MALE, 36

"I have this crazy habit. I can't help myself. About fifteen times a day, I automatically come out with bird calls. It's become a habit. Sometimes I talk to myself in bird language."

ELEVATOR STARTER, MALE, 27
(HE'S REALLY GOOD!)

My wife invites me to go out with her girlfriends when she has to go out of town. That way she knows who I'm with. In fact, I'm with my wife's girlfriend right now.

THEATRICAL DESIGNER, MALE, 30

I won't write with red or black ink. Any other color is fine. If someone hands me a pen that has red or black ink, I'll ask if they have another one. Those of my friends who are aware of my quirk automatically hand me an alternate color. I like red and black in just about anything else.

SECRETARY, FEMALE, 31

I turn on the TV as soon as I walk into my apartment regardless of what's on. It's a surrogate person.

NATIONAL AD MANAGER, CORPORATION, MALE, 30

As an act of civic pride and duty, I always stop at every *Don't Walk* sign and wait until the green *Walk* sign flashes. And, in fact, I admonish people who go against it as a sign of civil disobedience and irresponsibility. The city spends a great amount of money on the installation and maintenance of these devices, literally millions of dollars. The electricity is used twenty-four hours a day, 365 days a year. They have laws against jaywalking because of the hundreds of pedestrian deaths. But if you follow the law, people look at you like you're strange.

ATTORNEY, MALE, 38

My husband sits sideways to the television set and then turns his head to watch. It's the strangest thing.

TEACHER, FEMALE, 33
HER HUSBAND IS A BIOLOGY PROFESSOR, 37

My mother ironed all the rags and folded them neatly before she put them in the rag drawer. She was a meticulously clean woman who was very proud of the way she kept her house.

BOOK DESIGNER, FEMALE, 45
HER MOTHER WAS A HOUSEWIFE

A friend of mine grows a beard and shaves it off once a year. He saves the hair and keeps it in plastic bags, which he dates. Some people save string—he saves hair.

PRODUCT MANAGER, MALE, 28
HIS FRIEND IS A COURT OFFICER, 32

Frequently, when I'm on my way to the office, I'll suddenly think, "Did I lock the door?" And although I'm pretty certain that I did, there's a compulsion to get off the bus and go back to check which, in fact, I have done on several occasions. I always feel very silly because, of course, the door has always been locked.

STORE MANAGER, MALE, 56

Sometimes I go back downstairs to make sure that I turned the gas off, knowing inside that I already did. I'm constantly checking the gas stove, the car doors, my stereo and all on-off, open-close switches to make sure they're off. I've almost broken the knob on my stereo.

TRAFFIC COORDINATOR, AD AGENCY, MALE, 22

If I'm reading a good book, I don't want it to end so I stop reading about one to ten pages before the end and set it aside. I don't finish it until about a year later.

JR: *Do you remember the book after a year?*

I have a general idea and I reread some parts to fill in the gaps.

Ph.D., HISTORY OF TECHNOLOGY, FEMALE, 27

66 Some people, when they talk to you, will focus on a particular spot on your body—for example, your forehead or your chest. It's terribly disconcerting but I'm afraid that if I move, they may lose their train of thought. 99

OWNER, DIRECT MAIL BUSINESS, MALE, 53

In my family, when we send a letter to someone we're fond of, we turn the stamp upside down to signify an extra, added "I love you." We extend this to our boyfriends and girlfriends. My mother has written me a couple of letters without the stamp upside down and I've called her immediately afterwards asking if she hated me.

STUDENT, FEMALE, 20

If I'm walking down the left side of the street but my destination is on the right side, I will cross over, as soon as possible, to the side of the street where my destination is.

JR: *Why?*

I don't know, I just have a very strong feeling that I'd like to be on the side of the street where I'm going.

ART PROFESSOR, FEMALE, 28

I clean the rooms in the house in alphabetical order. I start with the bathroom, then I do the bedroom, then the kitchen and then the living room. That always seemed to me to be the best way to clean the house.

GRADUATE STUDENT, FEMALE, 24

I don't like going swimming but if I am anywhere where there is water nearby such as the ocean, bay, lake or any other body of water, I will take one dunk, completely submerging myself underneath. Usually I stall until the plane is about to leave and I wind up with wet underwear on the airplane.

EMERGENCY PHYSICIAN, MALE, 53

After I use a wet nap, I fold it up again and put it back in the envelope before discarding it. I've always been a very neat person.

COLLEGE ADMINISTRATOR, FEMALE, 29

Once I begin reading a book I have to finish it. It doesn't matter whether I like it or not.

OFFICE MANAGER FOR ORTHODONTIST, FEMALE, 52

Over the past ten years of car ownership, I've kept a detailed log every time I fill the car up with gas. I have a little record book that I keep in the glove compartment. Each time I fill the tank, I enter the mileage, the amount of gas I put in and the price and sometimes the name of the gas station, in the record book, but I've never used the information for any particular purpose. Everyone asks, "Why are you doing that?" And I say, "I don't know." And if people ask me, "How many miles do you get per gallon?," I have to admit that I have no idea. The reason I don't know is because I'm too lazy to take the record book out of the car and bring it into the house to analyze it.

ATTORNEY, FEMALE, 50-PLUS

Before I shut the TV off, I switch it back to channel 7, ABC, in New York, because that's the station I watch primarily, and that's where I'll want to begin watching the next day.

RETIRED DENTAL TECHNICIAN, FEMALE, 78

After I've been out somewhere, I look in the mirror when I come back in the house to see how I looked to other people.

NURSE, FEMALE, 39

It just kills me to put the first piece of garbage in a clean garbage bag. In fact, many times I find myself running to the incinerator with one wrapper or one can or a banana peel so I don't have to dirty the clean bag.

MASSEUSE, 58

❝ I smoke cigarettes backwards with the lighted part in my mouth because it feels good. It's impossible to burn yourself if you know the proper method which I've mastered over a period of many years. **❞**

PIANIST, MALE, 25

When I'm driving I don't like to hit my brakes because I don't want to wear them out so I try to keep going. When I see cars stalled in traffic, I change lanes, if I can, rather then step on the brakes.

MANAGER, AEROSPACE ENGINEERING, FEMALE, 39

I'm very nearsighted. Not only do I see better with my eyeglasses, I also hear better with them. I think it's because we all subconsciously lip-read to some extent and without my glasses, of course, I can't see the lip movements as well. But my quirk is that if the telephone rings, and I don't have my glasses on, I must run and quickly find them before I answer because otherwise I won't hear as well over the phone! That doesn't make any sense because, naturally, you can't lip-read over the phone.

DESKTOP PUBLISHER, FEMALE, 28

I turn off all the sounds, alerts and beeps on my computer. I just want silence. Let me work.

INTERNET STRATEGIST, MALE, 28

My wife gets upset because I always park in the farthest, most remote boondocks of a parking lot and we often have to walk a half a mile to get to the store. I try to find the most isolated location with the fewest cars so my car doesn't get dented. My car is six years old but the age of the car is irrelevant—this is how I feel comfortable no matter how long I've had the car.

VICE PRESIDENT, TEXTILE COMPANY, MALE, 46

Even if the elevator has arrived and the door is already open, my colleague at work must press the button. Each and every time—there has never been an exception.

EXECUTIVE RECRUITER FOR THE TECHNOLOGY INDUSTRY, MALE, 50s
HIS COLLEAGUE IS AN EXECUTIVE RECRUITER FOR THE TECHNOLOGY
INDUSTRY, MALE, 55

OFF-CENTER AND UNBALANCED

If I turn around to say hello to somebody, I have to turn around the other way to unwind. Or, if the telephone cord twirls around my leg or body, rather than just step out of it, I have to untwirl the other way.

GRADUATE STUDENT, FEMALE, 22

When I leave for work in the morning and I get a kiss on the cheek from my husband, I always turn my head around to the other side so he can plant a kiss on the exact same spot on my other cheek. If he misses the spot, I move my face around until he gets it in exactly the same spot. I always have to be even.

CPA, FEMALE, 51

If I close one eye, I have to close the other eye to make sure they both open and close the same amount of times.

FILM EDITOR, MALE, 32

I have to feel symmetrical at all times. If I put a hair clip on one side of my head, there has to be another one in the same place on the other side. If I scratch one arm, I scratch the same spot on the other arm. I just need to have the same feeling in the same area on each side, otherwise I feel unequal.

REGISTERED NURSE, FEMALE, 34

If I touch my right leg then I have to touch my left leg twice and then I have to go back to my right leg and touch it once so it's balanced. If I hear a note or part of a song and tap it out with my right hand, then I have to tap it out with my left hand twice and do it once again with my right hand for balance.

ASSISTANT TO TALENT AGENT, MALE, 25

HIGH AND FLIGHTY

Before I head to the airport, I thoroughly clean my apartment, especially the bathroom, and make sure it's immaculate in case I don't come back. I don't want anyone to come into a dirty apartment and say, "This is how that guy lived!"

PAPER CONE MANUFACTURER, MALE, 32

I check the year the plane was built before I get on. It's printed on the door to the plane. I already have my ticket and I get on anyway, but I figure if it's newer, it might stay up longer.

"SUMMER CHAIRMAN," INTERNET COMPANY, MALE, 23

I can't get on an airplane unless I call my mom and dad first. I just say, "Hello, I'm leaving now and this is the airline and the flight number." If the plane should crash, they'll know whether or not I was on that plane. If, for some reason, I'm unable to call them or I can't get them on the phone, I'm doubly nervous on the flight. It's a safety measure to call and give them all this information.

VICE PRESIDENT, INTERNATIONAL MARKETING, MALE, 31

Before I get on any plane I have to kiss my hand and tap on the side of the door a couple of times before I get on. I feel that if I'm giving a little love to the plane it will love me back and not crash.

ACCOUNT SPECIALIST, PUBLIC RELATIONS, MALE, 24

Whenever I board an airplane I always enter with my right foot. Someone once told me that doing that brings good luck. If there are stairs to climb, then as I approach the stairs, I count down from the top step to the bottom step—right, left, right, left—so I know how to begin ascending the flight of stairs to ensure that when I get to the top I'll board with my right foot for good luck.

LAWYER, MALE, 39

DIAL-A-QUIRK

I hang up the receiver of our wall phone upside down with the speaking part on the hanger. This way I know who used the phone last because my wife doesn't do it that way.

COURT OFFICER, MALE, 26

When I, or anyone else, hangs up our cordless telephone, I have to turn it back on, listen for the dial tone and turn it off again to make sure that the person is no longer on the other end and can't hear us going about the rest of our day.

TECHNICAL RECRUITER, FEMALE, 25

My mother changes the outgoing message on the answering machine every time she leaves the house. You have to be prepared for at least a three-minute message when you call her. The message reflects where she will be and lists every telephone number where she can be reached. It goes something like this, "Hi, I'm going to the store and then I'm going to the doctor and then I'm going to run a few errands but if you would like to reach me, you can try me at this number and if you can't get me there, you can always try my daughter and this is her number." When she goes on vacation, she'll leave everybody's contact information on the tape, including my brother's and my telephone numbers and at the end of it she'll say, "If you'd like to leave a message for our houseguest, please do so after the beep," to foil possible burglars.

MANAGER, AEROSPACE ENGINEERING, FEMALE, 39
HER MOTHER IS A RETIRED SECRETARY, 62

I never answer a telephone between rings, only in the process of a ring, because I assume people don't hang up in the middle of a ring. I don't. The caller is more likely to be on the other end.

MEDIA PLANNER, AD AGENCY, MALE, 26

Instead of putting names, addresses, and telephone numbers in an address book or palm device, I keep clusters of small pieces of paper, corners, cards, envelope flaps, etc., in my pocket. They may not look organized, but every time I pull out the entire wad, I can go right to the number I need!

FREELANCE MANAGER, MALE, 26

In a business situation I find myself standing up when I talk on the phone. And I'm not that short! It gives me a feeling of superiority and control over the situation.

VICE PRESIDENT, TEXTILE BUSINESS, MALE, 37

My friend has a psychological need to be the last one to hang up the phone. I only noticed it recently although I've known him for a long time. So now I play games with him. The close of the conversation goes something like this, Me: "Goodbye." Him: "Goodbye." Me: "See you." Him: "See you." Long pause. Me: "You still there?" But it's a losing battle. He'll just wait it out.

THEATER PUBLICIST, FEMALE, 28
HER FRIEND IS A SALESMAN, 34

SCORE

If you've checked over these other people and found yourself instead, score yourself as follows:

Twenty or less: Do you really expect me to believe that? You must be in denial.

Twenty-one to forty: Now we're talking. You're a world-class quirkster.

Over forty: I wouldn't admit that if I were you. Lie. And stop twirling your hair.

ABOUT THE AUTHOR

This time around, Judy Reiser is the designer, the publisher as well as the author of the current edition of *And I Thought I Was Crazy!* It was originally published by Simon & Schuster in 1980. Judy began collecting quirks after she and a friend had a conversation in which some of their own quirks were divulged and laughed about, and she soon discovered that everyone seemed to have quirks. She has been observing, gathering, intrigued with and laughing about quirks ever since then. Judy, a graphic designer, conceived and designed the merchandise in Crazy Stuff and the Katalin Media logo and Web site. She interviewed over 2,000 people for this book and for an upcoming sequel. She hopes that you have as much fun with this subject as she has.

Judy lives in New York with her husband, who insists that if she had written this book of quirks as an autobiography, it would have been much longer!

ABOUT THE ILLUSTRATOR

Randall Enos has been an illustrator since 1956. His work has appeared in *The New York Times*, *The Wall Street Journal*, *The Washington Post*, *Business Week*, *Money*, *Fortune*, *Forbes*, *Time*, *Newsweek*, *Boy's Life*, *Gourmet*, *Elektra Records* and *MacUser*. He has also done some advertising, record covers, children's books, film titles and calendars. Randy has lectured and taught at Parsons, Syracuse, Fairfield University, School of Visual Arts, the Philadelphia School of Art and Montclair in New Jersey.

Randy lives in Connecticut. And while he certainly sits to draw his illustrations, he always stands to eat his lunch. He inherited this quirk from his dad.

QUIRK QUEST

If you've observed a quirk or idiosyncrasy, in yourself or anyone else, that is amusing, strange, touching or a damn good idea, I'd love to hear about it for an upcoming sequel. Please include as many details as possible, as well as your gender, age and profession and the gender, age and profession of anyone involved. Also, please provide your contact information. Mail or e-mail it to:

Judy Reiser,
Katalin Media
236 East 47th Street
New York, NY 10017-2146

jreiser@katalinmedia.com

TO ORDER

For additional or multiple copies of this book check your local or online bookstore or:

Visit:
www.katalinmedia.com

Call:
1-800-431-1579

Crazy

FLAUNT YOU

**Toothpaste War
T-Shirt**
TS103
100% heavyweight
white cotton
Multi-Color Graphic
Sizes: M–XXL

You squeeze in the middle
I squeeze at the top
May this fight for supremacy
Not ever stop.

Blue Monday
the first day
of the work week

**Blue Monday
T-Shirt**
TS104
100% heavyweight
white cotton
Blue Graphic
Sizes: M–XXL

"And I
Thought
I Was
Crazy!"

**Crazy
T-Shirt**
TS105
100% heavyweight
white cotton
Multi-Color Graphic
Sizes: M–XXL

TO ORDER & FOR ADDITIONAL INFORMATION

TO SEE IN COLOR: VISI

© 2001 Judy Reiser. All Rights Reserved.